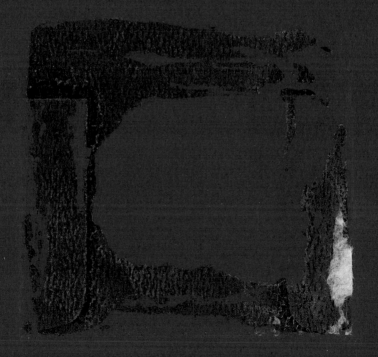

Thinking
Without Language

PSYCHOLOGICAL IMPLICATIONS OF DEAFNESS

Mephistopheles

Hear, therefore, one alone, for that is best, in sooth,
And simply take your master's words for truth.
On *words* let your attention center!
Then through the safest gate you'll enter
The temple-halls of Certainty.

Student

Yet in the word must some idea be.

Mephistopheles

Of course! But only shun too over-sharp a tension,
For just where fails the comprehension,
A word steps promptly in as deputy.
With words 'tis excellent disputing;
Systems to words 'tis easy suiting;
On words 'tis excellent believing;
No word can ever lose a jot from thieving.

Goethe

By no manner of make-believe can we discover the *what* of referents. We can only discover the *how*.

Ogden and Richards

HANS G. FURTH

Thinking

Without Language

PSYCHOLOGICAL IMPLICATIONS
OF DEAFNESS

The Free Press, New York

Collier-Macmillan Limited, London

Copyright © 1966 by Hans G. Furth

Printed in the United States of America

26394

Collier-Macmillan Canada, Ltd., Toronto, Ontario

Library of Congress Catalog Card Number: 66-10958

TO MY FRIENDS

T. G., *Vienna*
L. D., *Cornwall*
R. G., *Isle of Man*
B. C., *Sussex*
L. S., *Montreal*
M. S., *Ottawa*

Foreword

This book contains a variety of
topics, each of which could merit treatment in greater detail
and wider scope. It addresses itself to specialists in different
fields as well as to the ordinary intelligent reader. While I
conducted and described my work as an empirical psychologist
concerned with the thinking of deaf people, I realize that I
have ventured into areas that are the proper concern of philosophy, education, anthropology, linguistics, hearing and speech,
and rehabilitation. I may appear to have delved too deeply or
too superficially into areas depending on the specialized knowledge of the reader but I have tried to say nothing that is not
scientifically defensible. My concern is primarily with the vital
psychological reality of human thinking. In this pursuit I did
not hesitate to break with historically conditioned scientific
approaches that provide an inadequate conceptual environment for the questions and indeed the facts of the present
investigations.

The early chapters set the stage and clarify in a preliminary
fashion the questions to which subsequent chapters address
themselves. Both the experimental population and the questions

raised may be novel for the reader even though he holds many unanalyzed notions and stereotypes about them. Concerning the *deaf population* I initially ask the reader to accept some facts which will be documented later on in the book. The vast majority of deaf people, i.e., persons profoundly deaf from earliest childhood, do not know the native language of their country with any substantial degree of competence. Even a nonverbal system of manual signs is not readily available to most of the deaf during their formative years. Consequently the deaf child is in the unique position of having to grow up and develop intellectually without the benefit of the conventional system of language which is present to all hearing children. With regard to *language,* it is here always understood in a strict sense as referring to the natural, living language of a human society. As such it must be an organized system and must have extra-subjective reality in order to be shared by all the members of a society. These two points concerning the deaf and language will, of course, be explained at greater length in the course of the book, but this preliminary explanation may save some reader the trouble of reading large parts of the book with a different set or *Einstellung.*

The middle chapters relate a number of rather simple, straightforward experimental observations on the thinking of hearing and deaf people. A minimum of highly technical, methodological or statistical finesse is included. All of these studies have been described in detail in scientific journals and the interested reader is referred to these journal articles.

The final chapters seem to me to contain necessary implications from the empirical findings. They deal with the fundamental problem of a theory of thinking and language which would coordinate the findings and also with very practical problems raised by the actual state of affairs in the development and education of the deaf.

It is a pleasure to thank those who have contributed and helped me in the completion of the book. My thanks are due first to James Youniss and Bruce M. Ross, my colleagues at the Center who have lent a willing ear to my searchings and problems, who have cooperated along with my research effort and have reacted to successive stages of the manuscript with critical and constructive sympathy. I would also like to mention with appreciation the names of the following persons who have contributed by their work or counsel in this investigation: Robert M. Dowling, Norman A. Milgram, Ruben A. Mendez, James E. Ollson, Peter B. Pufall, Elizabeth M. Sheehan.

Most of the research described in these pages was in part aided by a research (RD 704) and training (198–T) grant from the Vocational Rehabilitation Administration, United States Department of Health, Education and Welfare. This agency deserves credit for being among the first concerned with the welfare of deaf people. I am grateful for the generous support received and the opportunity it provided to serve science and the welfare of the deaf.

Finally my thanks go to the schools, the clubs, the agencies and the many individual hearing and deaf persons of all ages who cooperated so willingly in this research project. With regard to hearing subjects, I would like to express my appreciation particularly to the School Board of Prince Georges County, Maryland, and the parochial schools in the Washington, D.C., area. For their cooperation in research with the deaf I am most appreciative to the following schools: Gallaudet College and Kendall School, D.C., New York School for the Deaf, and the following state schools for the deaf: Maryland, North Carolina, Oregon, Tennessee, Virginia, Washington, West Virginia.

Center for Research in Thinking and Language
The Catholic University of America
Washington, D.C., May 1965

Contents

haviorism — linguistic and philosophical contributions to the question — Whorf's linguistic relativism — operational definition — science of signs — distinct functions of signal and symbol — Morris — Langer.

6 approaches — 1) normative — 2) material, Skinner, "verbal" learning — 3) mediating, Osgood, verbal mediation — 4) linguistic, Chomsky — 5) pathological, aphasia — 6) "neo-behavioral" — England: Bartlett — U.S.A.: Mowrer, Bruner — Russia: Vygotsky, Luria — Werner's organismic-developmental approach.

Obstacles to be overcome — nonverbal task defined — nonverbal methods to study thinking — standardized "tests" and experimental tasks — tasks of discovery and transfer — 5 areas of thinking to be investigated.

Experiment 1: *Sameness, Symmetry, and Opposition*—with deaf and hearing children — experiment 2: *A Replication of Experiment 1 with Retarded Children* — experiment 3: *Discovery of Similarities*—with deaf, retarded and normal children — experiment 4: *Conceptual Discovery and Control*—the Part-Whole concept with deaf and hearing children.

Experiment 5: *Visual Memory Span*—with deaf and hearing adolescents and adults — experiment 6: *Gestalt Laws in Visual Perception*—with deaf and hearing children and adolescents.

Experiment 7: *Conservation of Weight*—with deaf and hearing children — experiment 8: *Conservation of Amount of Liquid*—with deaf and hearing children and adolescents.

Experiment 9: *Classification Transfer*—with deaf and hearing college students — experiment 10: *Conceptual Performance in Deaf Adults* — with deaf and hearing adults — experiment 11:

Logical Symbol Discovery and Use—with deaf and hearing adults and children.

tence in deaf children — the "verbal" overemphasis of general education — educational problems of linguistically deficient children — a curriculum to foster thinking non-verbally — demonstration of teaching of logical thinking to deaf children.

The Problem

My association with the deaf began with two years of work in connection with a New York State mental health project studying deaf families and persons living, not in a school, but in the community at large.

I believe I was fortunate in this introduction, as it gave me a better chance to gain a reality-oriented approach in my subsequent psychological work with the deaf than if I had been associated with them only in the school environment. In this way I was able to observe the deaf adult as he is in his everyday life; working, engaging in social life, and raising a family.

In the course of this research project with the deaf, I was constantly impressed by the obvious fact that they were very poor in language ability. Simple language had to be used in communicating with them, and it would have been easy to assume from this that the deaf were incapable of abstract thought which is so closely identified with verbal thought.

However, I had observed that the life of the mature deaf seems to differ only minimally from the adult life of the hearing person. Apparently both hearing and deaf persons are motivated by similar values, show interest in similar questions,

1

and engage in similar recreational and professional activities. This is not to say there are no noticeable differences between the deaf and hearing in general: for example, the tendency of the deaf to seek each other's company and the small range of occupations to which they are generally limited.

A number of questions came to mind: Are these differences due to a way of thinking peculiar to the deaf, or may they be explained by the fact that deaf persons have not been informed of many things that the average hearing person learns, not through formal training, but merely through experience and social contact? In the sphere of social relations, could some so-called shortcomings be traced to the necessarily limited and artificial nature of the deaf person's exchange with his environment? To what extent is his personality, and consequently his thinking, shaped by the emotional effects of his handicap and the fact that many of his early years have been spent in the sheltered and therefore necessarily confined environment of a residential school for the deaf? Would it be possible to teach nonverbally some of the information and ideas which the deaf seem to lack, to aid them in reaching fuller mental and emotional development at an earlier age?

Such considerations prompt one to inquire whether the differences observed in deaf people's behavior are traceable to a different cognitive structure which they develop because they lack language. How should one describe a cognitive structure? To what cause should one ascribe deficiencies which make the deaf appear "concrete-minded"? Apparently, it is much easier for a deaf person to learn the vocabulary of things and objects physically observable, whose attributes may be demonstrated by action, than to comprehend the verbal subtleties of, for example, "purpose" or "democracy."

Furthermore, I was struck by the contrast between the deaf adult and the deaf child I later came to know in their school environment. In the latter the picture is much different! Many deaf children prove failures, or near-failures, in academic subjects. The time required for them to cover the usual primary and secondary education is much longer as a rule than for the average child. Observing these children who have so much difficulty with ordinary school subjects, one could not imagine them ever growing up to live normal adult lives. Yet they do just that! Could this startling change be attributed to the fact that the whole scholastic curriculum is based upon verbal skill while real life does not depend so exclusively upon it? These questions and related ones about the place of language in mature thinking lead the psychological researcher to consider whether the all-important stress placed upon verbal learning by teachers of the deaf is altogether advantageous.

This question is raised with full appreciation of the historical developments which have led to the verbal emphasis in the teaching of the deaf. In fact, it is the logical result of rather vague theoretical notions and assumptions of the past. For many centuries the deaf were considered lacking in normal intelligence because they could not speak. Consequently, when an effort was undertaken to help them, it was based on the hypothesis that only if they could be taught to speak would their handicap be overcome. This agreed with the assumption that ability to use language was the gauge of human intelligence and that language was indeed the key to all that is abstract and conceptually mature in man.

Such an apparently abstruse problem as the interrelation between language and thinking seemed to lie outside the empirical realm and thus held no interest for most investigators. Even with the advent of empirical methods in psychology, this question of the relation of language and knowledge failed to elicit interest. The empirical psychologist wished at all costs to avoid speculation and was careful to discard not only the principles but even the topics of philosophy.

In general, therefore, most American psychologists have avoided studying human thinking. Only recently has a lively interest been shown in such questions, and this has come about

3

partly because verbal behavior was recognized as lying validly within the scope of psychological investigation.

With the recognition of language behavior as a valid sphere of psychological interest, thinking also became a proper subject of scientific investigation. Until very recently, little or no attempt has been made to define and distinguish notions in the language-thinking area. This omission was in part due to the indifference of investigators to whether the behavior studied was termed language or thinking. It may also be partially attributed to the fact that in all these investigations certain unspecified assumptions were accepted without question.

Among these assumptions may have been the theory that language faithfully mirrors thinking, that language is almost the only important symbol system, and that language, symbols, and thinking are necessarily, even inseparably linked. The terms "abstract" and "concrete" were used in rather loose fashion and verbal behavior was vaguely identified with abstract or conceptual behavior while nonverbal behavior was associated with concrete behavior on a perceptual level.

As to the relation between language and thinking, there are two viewpoints from which an investigation of deaf persons may be approached. One approach is to begin with the assumption that a necessary relation does exist. I feel that most observation of deaf people's thought to date has been undertaken from this angle. I also feel that the psychologist's contribution to this field of research might be much greater if he took the second approach of holding no preconceived ideas on the dependency of thinking on language.

From my own experience with deaf adults and from some preliminary first findings, it seemed more scientific to start with the second hypothesis: namely, to expect no difference in cognitive structure between the hearing and the deaf. Ideally the starting hypothesis should make no difference in the scientific procedure, but because of the unavoidable human factor, "the way a question is asked limits and disposes the ways in which any answer—right or wrong—may be given. . . . In this way the intellectual treatment of any datum, any experience, any subject, is determined by the nature of our question and only carried out in the answers." (Langer, 1964, p. 15–16)

Thus those who have hypothesized differences in the thinking of the deaf usually employed verbal tests and found their theory borne out as they observed that deaf persons were in general poorer than hearing persons in such tasks.

Yet it should be immediately obvious to the impartial observer that such results might simply indicate the already well-known poverty of the deaf in language. For those investigators, however, verbal expression was equated with abstract thinking. Therefore, the results of their tests provided supportive evidence, if such were needed, that deaf persons achieve a lower level of verbal expression than the hearing.

Let us examine this assumption more closely. Is thinking really nothing more than *verbal* thinking? One is often impressed by the fact that much of the verbal communication among the hearing is nothing more than a display of linguistic habits carrying little thought content, even being used frequently to conceal unacceptable social behavior. Would it be possible to separate the two phenomena and study thinking without language? It was to throw light on this question that the investigations reported in this book were undertaken.

Several related developments supported the opinion that an empirical appraisal of the role of language in cognitive development would be especially opportune at this time. Aside from popular notions on the subject, and the fact that the average teacher, parent or man in the street may have rather definite opinions about the necessity of language for manifesting intellective behavior, the following considerations made such a study apropos:

(1) The cultural theories of Whorf and Sapir have proved and are still proving a useful basis for numerous experiments in linguistics.

(2) A renewed interest in cognitive development, as indicated in the extensive studies of such investigators as Piaget, Werner, Bruner, and others, makes it imperative to observe and meaningfully relate nonverbal and verbal behavior in the growing child.

(3) The recent rapprochement of the trends noted in points 1 and 2 has given rise to the new science of psycholinguistics, a specialized field of psychological endeavor expressly devoted to shedding light on problems of linguistic behavior.

(4) A fertile sphere of experimentation and theorizing centers around the work of behaviorist studies of verbal learning by Skinner, Osgood, and others.

(5) Last, and most important from this writer's viewpoint, we have among us many deaf children as well as other speech-handicapped individuals whose plight commands our best efforts and whose needs must be met.

One of the purposes of this work, then, is to present some theoretical implications of a number of empirical studies which have a direct bearing on the role of language and its relation to thinking behavior. It will include recently completed and some ongoing investigations with deaf and hearing persons conducted at The Catholic University of America's Center for Research in Thinking and Language.

It is hoped by means of this evidence to throw light on three key questions:

(1) What is the effect of language-deprivation on the intellectual development of the deaf?

(2) What conclusions can we draw from these results for an empirically-based view on the language-thinking relation?

(3) What is the significance of these findings for theories of thinking and what implications can we derive for educational practices with deaf children and hearing children as well?

CHAPTER II

The Deaf and Their Language

The history of the deaf has yet to be written. We know little about them in the past, and what we do know reflects more the hearing person's prejudices and unenlightened attitudes than the actual life and feelings of the deaf themselves. Because deafness is an invisible disability manifesting itself mainly in failure to communicate, hearing people cannot readily understand the effects of this handicap, and even scientific investigators are faced with a serious and unfamiliar obstacle.

When we speak here of the deaf, we refer specifically to those whose hearing loss prevents, for all practical purposes, auditory contact with the world around them, and has done so either from birth or since before the acquisition of language. Such persons are distinguished from those who have lost their hearing after establishment of language facility, and from the hard-of-hearing who have some functional reception of auditory communication.

Scholars and ordinary people, in fact society in general, traditionally considered the deaf to be on a subhuman level, incapable of education or culture, bereft of human intelligence.

7

It was inconceivable to our ancestors that man could develop beyond the most primitive level without the aid of language.

Only within the last few hundred years has this view changed, and then it changed through an economic rather than a humanitarian motive. Under existing laws, deaf sons could not inherit their fathers' estates. To prevent property from passing out of family control, a Spanish nobleman of the late 16th century hired a private tutor for his deaf heir. This tutor succeeded in teaching his pupil to read, write, and even to speak. Having proved by his use of speech that he was indeed a human being, the young man was able to claim his inheritance. Thus was set the pattern which still persists today—the emphasis on language alone in teaching the deaf, and the contingent assumption that language is essential for thinking as well as for speech.

At the time of the French Revolution the first free school for the deaf was opened, and what had been the privilege of a few rich families became the recognized responsibility of the community. Eventually all developed countries offered free and public education for the deaf. In the United States today about 90 per cent of the estimated total of deaf children attend special schools and classes and for the great majority these schools for the deaf are the sole source of all formal education.

Discovery that the deaf were educable—that they were in fact normal apart from their deafness—did not immediately dispel the effects of ignorance and superstitious prejudice, but it did give rise to many efforts to lessen the burdens of severe auditory handicap. Along with these efforts came scientific studies of causes of deafness and the influence of such factors as heredity, birth injuries, disease, and illnesses during pregnancy. Even today, our knowledge about the process of hearing and the specific nature of deafness is inadequate. The need for audiological research is urgent.

In the past the deaf have been commonly referred to as "deaf-mute," a term denoting inability to speak and comprehend spoken language. Today we merely use the term "deaf," realizing that the addition of the accidental adjective is as unbecoming as if we spoke of a blind person who had difficulty moving about as a "blind-immobile."

Even today, despite all the progress that has been made, the deaf are known only to a few "outsiders." Largely excluded by their communication handicap from ordinary society, they naturally tend to group together and form their own "community" within the wider society. Among themselves they communicate in the "language of signs," a system of conventional manual symbols supplemented by some finger spelling. We refer to it here as sign language, with emphasis on the fact that it is not a dialect form of English or of any other verbal language. It consists rather of visible movements of the hands or arms, many of them derived from natural gestures. Sign language as used in the United States may be historically traced to manual symbols introduced into this country from France in 1816 at the time when the first United States school for the deaf was founded at Hartford, Connecticut. Sign language is no longer formally taught in any school but is acquired by the deaf child by association with other deaf persons.

Nevertheless, it is a living language and fulfills its primary function of providing a means of communication. While books are available which list in vocabulary fashion the signs for the names of things and for single expressions, a study of the structure or syntax of sign language remains for some interested linguist or anthropologist.

As distinct from signing, finger spelling is nothing but a form of writing and must be used when no conventional symbol is available; for example, in proper names or with unfamiliar objects and concepts. However, the use of manual spelling, like reading and writing, presupposes knowledge of the verbal language and generally the deaf are not proficient in it, as will be demonstrated shortly.

To communicate with the hearing, writing is the most used and most reliable method employed by the deaf. Contrary to general popular opinion, very few deaf persons are expert lip readers. Some have a limited facility in it but the great majority cannot master it at all. A similar statement can be made with regard to speech. Both speech and lip reading assume of course a basic familiarity with the language. As our main interest in this investigation centers on language as linguistic competence, rather than on speech or lip reading, more will be said about the language achievement of the deaf later on.

The number of deaf people in the United States is now estimated to be close to 200,000. The typical deaf adult is married to a deaf spouse and has a stable place of employment. While most deaf persons of working age are employed, relatively few hold professional or technical positions and few are known to have attained great prominence in any field. They tend toward occupations in which the ability to communicate is not of major importance. Children of deaf couples can usually hear; deaf children are found more frequently in families with hearing parents.

The deaf have a busy social life among themselves; many belong to clubs and they enjoy traveling and visiting one another. Deaf Americans are proud of being independent taxpaying citizens. When Congress some years ago planned to introduce an amendment granting the deaf tax privileges similar to those extended to the blind, the National Association of the Deaf earnestly requested and succeeded in bringing about withdrawal of the motion.

In general, an unbiased observer cannot help being impressed by the deaf group in our population, particularly if he expects that without a natural verbal language one can hardly live a mature or constructive life. This observation should not, however, lead to the impression that the lives of the deaf have in general no serious shortcomings which need improvement. By comparison with the hearing members of our society, the deaf are frequently under-educated and similarly under-employed. As might be expected, they hold a greater proportion of low-paying, low-status jobs than the general population and their opportunities for advancement are limited. Then too, there are numerous individual cases in which deaf persons live an isolated existence or neglect family or civic obligations. However, these circumstances certainly are not unique among the deaf. Most recent careful investigations have failed to provide conclusive evidence which would seriously question the basic normality of the social, emotional, and civic life of our deaf population (cf. Bobrove, 1964; Furfey and Harte, 1964; Rainer, Altshuler, Kallman and Deming, 1963).

What is the usual experience of a child born deaf, from birth until he becomes an adult member of the deaf community? Typically, he is the child of hearing parents who do not suspect any disability until around the age of one to one-and-a-half when the child does not show the normal beginnings of speech. The pediatrician may send him to a speech and hearing clinic for audiometric tests, but more frequently he will try to allay the anxiety of the parents, advising them to wait a few months to see if their child is merely a late talker. Even if the audiologist is consulted, a definite diagnosis before the age of three is not always an easy matter.

Consequently during a long period of infancy and early childhood the deaf child's parents watch ever more anxiously for any encouraging signs, meanwhile receiving all kinds of well-meant if often conflicting advice from both professional and lay sources. A clinical psychologist may be asked to test the child's intelligence level to rule out a possible connection between muteness and mental deficiency. A psychiatrist may be called upon to offer his opinion about infantile autism. A neurologist may give the child clinical tests to determine the functioning of nervous connections. Relatives and friends meanwhile are adding their opinions to the confusion. At

11

last, perhaps by age three, it may be finally established that the child has a severe hearing loss which makes it impossible for him to hear or discriminate sounds so as to learn language in the natural way.

If the parents live near a speech and hearing clinic, the child will probably then be enrolled in a nursery class for a limited number of hours each week to begin speech training. The child with residual hearing will be encouraged to use a hearing aid if that proves helpful. The emphasis is on speech and understanding speech by lip reading.

At age six or earlier, the child may be enrolled in a regular school for the deaf. It may be a day school, if he lives sufficiently close to one, but in many cases it is a residential school some distance from home. Henceforth the child will be separated from his family for a good part of the year. Not surprisingly, he often comes to feel more secure in the school than with his own family which does not understand him and cannot communicate with him satisfactorily. Significantly, the majority of deaf children of hearing parents achieve only a minimum of articulated communication with others during their earliest years—crucial years in the development of personality with all that this term entails.

The primary aim of all schools for the deaf is to teach language, with particular emphasis on speech and lip reading, or more properly, speech reading. This approach is referred to as the "oral" method. The use of any kind of manual symbols is prohibited in a few oral schools of the purist type, while in the average residential school a kind of reasonable compromise prevails. There the lower grade pupils are uniformly exposed to oral teaching only, and are frequently kept separate from older pupils. At about age twelve, the child moves into the intermediate grades and meets older pupils from whom he learns the manual symbols outside the classroom. Eventually, he may be placed in a so-called vocational curriculum where the emphasis is no longer on speech and the instructor may use whatever means of communication is most likely to be successful, including formal signs, if he is familiar with them.

Many deaf pupils remain in the school until they are eighteen or even twenty years of age. For the relatively few deaf students who master verbal language, Gallaudet College in Washington, D.C., is the preferred place of advanced study. Specifically conducted for the benefit of deaf students, Gallaudet has classes conducted by the simultaneous method of speech and signing. However, very few young deaf people attend college or receive any higher education.

It is impossible to convey adequately the oral-manual controversy permeating the education of the deaf without discussing historical events and methodological arguments which do not belong in this book. Educators of the oralist school contend that we must prepare the deaf child for a full life in the hearing society and that linguistic competence is an unavoidable prerequisite for this life. This controversy need not detain us at this point. The fact is that under our present educational system the vast majority of persons, born deaf, *do not acquire functional language competence,* even after undergoing many years of intensive training.

Here are the results of a recent investigation of language comprehension of deaf pupils. The data were collected in May 1959 on all pupils age 10 to 16 in 73 schools for the deaf in the United States and Canada. The Reading Test of the Metropolitan Achievement Tests Elementary Battery, suitable for Grades 3 and 4, was administered to 5307 pupils (excluding 392 pupils with reported IQ below 75) and norms of the results were computed and tabulated by the publisher of the test. The special deaf norms, based on an imposing 54 per cent of the total deaf population in that age range, were published by Wrightstone, Aronow, and Moskowitz (1962) and are compared in Table 1 with the norms for the national hearing sample.

Table 1—Silent Reading Achievement of Deaf Pupils Compared to Grade Equivalent of Hearing Norms

Age	N	Mean Raw Score and Standard Deviation	Mean Grade Equivalent	Median Grade Equivalent	Percentage Scoring at Grade 4.9 or Above
10½–11½	654	12.6 (8.1)	2.7	2.6	1%
11½–12½	849	14.9 (8.5)	2.8	2.7	2%
12½–13½	797	17.6 (9.1)	3.1	3.1	6%
13½–14½	814	18.7 (9.3)	3.3	3.2	7%
14½–15½	1035	20.8 (9.3)	3.4	3.3	10%
15½–16½	1075	21.6 (9.5)	3.5	3.4	12%

The results, showing that between the ages of 10 and 16 the deaf on the average did not advance even one full grade in reading ability, confirm what is common knowledge to anyone working with the deaf whether here or abroad. The profoundly deaf person who has been so since before the age of language learning may know quite a number of isolated words, but with rare exceptions will he be able to form or comprehend sentences or paragraphs which approximate the complexity of Grade 4 reading level.

The linguistic deficiency of the deaf consists more precisely in their inability to handle linguistic ordering or structure. Reading tests below the Grade 4 level are recognized as sampling only fragmentary aspects of the living language. Thus comprehension of Grade 4 reading as measured by present standardized tests may be proposed as a criterion of linguistic competence.

According to this criterion, the percentage of deaf pupils who have linguistic competence, as can be seen in Table 1, reaches a maximum of only 12 per cent, a number which may be somewhat inflated by the presence of pupils in the norming sample who had lost their hearing after the acquisition of language, or who were not profoundly deaf. In any case, this normative investigation demonstrates that one can hardly assert that deaf people are "at home" in the language they have striven to learn for so many years.

It should be noted that a 14 year old deaf youngster with a reading level of Grade 3 is not comparable to a hearing peer who may have difficulty in reading. The hearing individual enjoys a comfortable mastery of the language even though he may be retarded in reading. For the deaf, on the other hand, the reading level *is* the ceiling of linguistic competence. It is quite inappropriate to designate this latter condition as retardation in reading. It is properly termed incompetence or deficiency in verbal language, a condition very rare among the hearing but almost universal among the deaf. The occasional deaf adult who is thoroughly at home in English has either lost his hearing after the establishment of language or does not have so serious a hearing loss as to be justifiably classified among the deaf, or, finally, he may be an exception. For all practical purposes, however, the typical deaf person, whether child or adult, is a language-deficient person both in his present functioning and in his past experience.

Linguistic competence denotes mastery of the basic structure of a language. We know what linguistic competence is, although experts have not arrived at a thorough understanding of the specific sub-skills comprising this remarkable achievement. It is granted that a certain number of vocabulary items are an implicit part of it, but one can readily understand that mastery of the sequential ordering and syntactical modifications of words are even more important aspects of linguistic competence. In this respect a four-year-old hearing child masters language and so does an adult with an IQ level of 40. In hearing persons therefore, language learning does not necessarily presuppose a high intelligence level. Many persons whom we do not consider capable of complex intelligent behavior learn the language of our society better than the majority of pupils in our schools for the deaf. The true "language" of the deaf is the sign language, as one can readily observe.

15

It is not surprising that the deaf themselves are somewhat resentful toward the society that constantly tells them they should not live and communicate as they do, but should learn the speech of society and mix freely with the hearing. They feel instinctively that without sign language most of them would indeed be unable to communicate anything but the most primitive and obvious needs. There would be no possibility of forming a meaningful community based purely on verbal exchanges. It is therefore in the deaf community that the deaf person finds opportunity for social, emotional, and intellectual development and fulfillment.

In the present investigation, we turned for our linguistically deficient subjects to schools and clubs for the deaf where no particular policy of selection is practiced. Excluding those who had lost their hearing after the acquisition of language, it was not difficult to find the kind of deaf person described in the foregoing paragraphs.

It would be naïve in any overall study not to take into account kinds of hearing loss, time of onset, the presence of other disabling conditions, personal history, personality traits, and other factors which may have a bearing on intellectual and linguistic development. However, this first attempt at studying the thinking processes of the deaf proceeds according to the following working hypothesis:

A sample of typically deaf persons is chosen according to chronological age and some other obvious criteria. Their behavior is observed on a task of thinking which provides meaningful data when given to hearing subjects. If performance of the deaf and hearing differ only minimally, there is no need to scrutinize the deaf sample for factors on which subjects in it may differ. If, on the other hand, the deaf prove inferior on a given task, we must look for some condition shared by all or a majority of the deaf which has a specific relation to the inferior performance.

CHAPTER III

Preliminary Clarifications

           In order to contribute to some clarification in the understanding of thinking behavior in the deaf or the hearing, it would seem imperative first to agree on a number of terms. Such preliminary observations are not intended to be dogmatic or explanatory statements. Not everyone may agree on the appropriateness of the terminology. The reader may not readily see the reason for some of the following statements. His indulgence is asked in weighing the historical and empirical evidence subsequent chapters will provide.

Our concern will be with four key words and their meaning: language and the related term, linguistic competence; concept; symbol; thinking. Because of the diffuse meanings these words convey, it is imperative to clarify them at the outset. Otherwise we should find ourselves using words which have different meanings for different readers, and what is worse, different meanings in different contexts.

However, more than a simple clarification of lexical meaning is involved, since these are the very notions to be empirically investigated. No researcher in this area can afford to feel superior to so-called philosophical speculations and concentrate simply on observable facts. Each notion to be discussed is laden with philosophical theories reaching back through the centuries. There is no alternative. We cannot accept uncritically the theoretical assumptions embodied in our everyday use of language. We must attempt to analyze meanings. This course requires sifting mental or linguistic constructs from the reality on which they are based.

The term "language" is here taken in the narrow sense of the natural, verbal language of a society. It does not include all systems of communication or signals, nor does it encompass formally taught symbols, such as mathematics or symbolic logic. It refers here to the quite specific denotation of mother tongue, the language of a society which practically all human infants are exposed to and learn by the time they are four years old.

"Linguistic competence" refers to the specific skill of the person who has learned a language. A minimum criterion of linguistic competence is an implicit comprehension of linguistic structure. Reading and writing and even speaking are thus not necessary components of linguistic competence. Insofar as oral language is difficult to "measure" and comprehension of oral language even more so, there is no ready test available which would quantify linguistic competence without confounding it with variables more properly related to intelligence. This is illustrated by the fact that vocabulary cannot simply be employed as a test of linguistic competence. A vocabulary score is usually the best single indicator of "intelligence level" as measured by standardized IQ tests. Standard measures of language behavior rightly concentrate on syntactical criteria, on the complexity and successive ordering of the words, in short, on linguistic structure. Because single words are insufficient indicators of linguistic competence and the natural structure of the language is not adequately represented in reading tests below Grade 4 level, it was proposed in Chapter II to employ success on standardized reading tests corresponding to Grade 4, as a tentative criterion only for those nonoral persons in whom linguistic competence is questionable. For children who are not deaf, evidence is usually abundant that they are "at home" in their mother tongue, though all may not use it in an equally correct, intelligent, or interesting way.

"Concept" is here understood as an abstract term referring to a characteristic of thinking behavior, insofar as it lends itself to discursive verbalization. What is called a concept may or may not be verbalized by the thinking person, who may or may not be explicitly aware of it. In the context of our inquiry, the word "concept" is not to be a priori identified with verbal concept. When it is said here that a person has attained or transferred a concept, this does not imply that he is aware of the principle or that he knows the verbal expression for that concept. It merely means that the observed behavior is adequately, if not always helpfully, described in our language by the expression: "The person has a concept." In objective reality, concepts are not something apart from the behaving person, or in James' words, "separate subjective entities that come and go" (James, 1950, Vol. 1, p. 196).

We know that illness does not exist apart from people who are ill. Ill people are real; illness is an abstract term under which we include the characteristic symptoms of a person who is ill. The concept of illness refers then to the ill state of a biological organism just as the term "concept" itself refers to the knowing or thinking behavior of a living person. Both terms, illness and concept, have no separate existence apart from persons who are ill or who think.

The distinction made above may appear trivial. It will be pointed out that scientists and physicians are not much troubled by the fact that we speak as though illness was a separate entity acquired by the person who becomes sick. They know this is merely a matter of speaking. Unfortunately, things are more complicated in the area of thinking and concepts. Granted that a concept has no reality apart from persons who know the concept and behave accordingly, our language entangles us now further by the expression: "We know a concept; we think a concept." This added separation of knowing or thinking from the notion of concept has been chiefly responsible for more philosophical debates throughout the history of Western culture than perhaps any other single factor. It has been suggested that much of our Western philosophy, whatever else it may be, is but a footnote to Plato's speculations on the nature of ideas.

We agree readily enough that concepts are not entities outside the thinking person, but we continue to speak of concepts as if they were the objects of thinking. In other words, we separate thinking from concepts. It is this separation or reification of concepts, as if they were independent units, elements or objects of thinking which has proved an obstacle to philosophical or empirical investigations of thinking or conceptual behavior. The expression "to think in concepts" implies as artificial a distinction between thinking and concepts as the expression "to have a concept" implies a false separation of person and concept. A person who solves a mathematical problem is said to think, or to apply mathematical principles. These principles or concepts, however, are not something apart from his actual thinking on the problem.

A "person who is ailing with a sickness" refers to the same reality as the "person who has the sickness," which in turn refers to the "sick person." No one would be tempted to make sickness the real object of ailing, even though our language does so. Concepts with regard to thinking should be considered as steps in walking. A tall person may "have a long step" and "take long steps" when he walks. The reality to be investigated is the walking behavior and not the step. If some one wanted to study the steps in which the tall man walks, we would expect him to be a companion of Alice in Wonderland.

Perhaps this can be clarified further by our use of the word "perception." From the present viewpoint, the sentence: "A person perceives a perception"; is interpreted in the same way as the sentence: "A person thinks a concept." Why is it that we commonly reify one but not the other? Why is percept or perception easily recognized as an abstract term for the end product of perceiving, while concept is thought of as having some objective reality apart from thinking? It is probably because the reference of perception is present to our sense and consequently there is little temptation to reify any subjective process. For the same reason that we tend to objectify concepts, we are naïvely inclined to regard perception as being naturally "out there," something real to which receptors merely have to pay attention in order for it to be noticed and registered as perception.

On the other hand, the object to which a concept refers is not only not always present, but frequently defies any objective presentation. Who can easily point to an object illustrating the concept "purpose" or "difference"? Even in the case of a concept like "triangle," readily illustrated by any number of possible triangles, one is no longer able, as in the case of the percept, to assert that the concept has its full reality in a triangle which can be seen, or in a subjective image of that triangle. Consequently, we tend to reify the concept in the symbol. The name or verbal symbol has become the preferred basis for understanding the reality of a concept. Hence the frequent theoretical confusion of concept with verbal concept, and the identification of symbol, particularly the verbal symbol, with concept or thinking.

In this book the word "concept" is to be understood as an artificial, abstracted unit of thinking behavior. In fact, one can always substitute the word "thinking" for concept. When, for instance, later on we speak of the concept of "sameness" or "disjunction," we could as well say "thinking sameness" or "disjunctive thinking." Any thinking behavior—that is, anything whatsoever—can be given a name and pose as a concept. This is perhaps a convenient linguistic usage but it should not lead us to assume that concepts are separate objects from thinking. Neither need we accept a priori that the name is an inherent part of the concept. We leave this question open and wait for evidence from the conceptual behavior of deaf persons.

An understanding of the term "symbol" is here approached from the viewpoint of the thinking person. It is used in connection with some explicit object or event, something one can designate (e.g., the sound of a voice or the movement of the hand), or at least something experienced as similar to an outside event (e.g., image, dream). This symbolic object or event derives its meaning, not from what it is in itself, but from its reference to a thinking state, i.e., from its symbolic function. In short, where there is a symbol there is the question of thinking and of meaning. Not every learned stimulus or stimulus substitute is here called a symbol but only such objects or events that directly refer to or represent a state of knowing or thinking.

With these restrictions, one can distinguish symbol first from internal representation in the wide sense. As Piaget proposes:

Let us first clearly define our terms. We use the word "representation" in two different senses. In its broad sense, representation is identical with thought, i.e., with all intelligence which is based on a system of concepts or mental schemas and not merely on perceptions and actions. In its narrow sense, representation is restricted to the mental or memory image, i.e., the symbolic evocation of absent realities (Piaget, 1962, p. 67).

Insofar as it involves an internal transforming or processing of objective reality, thinking as such is sometimes said to represent or symbolize reality. However, this is not a formal use of the word "symbol," since thinking, as internally organizing, is not something explicit and distinct from what it refers to, as a symbol must be. Thinking and the object-thought-about are one and the same reality, while a true symbol is distinct from the thing to which it refers.

The second distinction we wish to make is between a symbol and a signal. A symbol refers to thinking or a concept; a signal may substitute for a stimulus and anticipates or triggers an action. This distinction rests entirely upon the difference between knowing an object and reacting to an object. More will be said about this in Chapter XIII.

"Thinking" is the key term in the discussion on concept and symbol. Again referring to a fuller development in Chapter XIII, one can assert that thinking is any activity which is related to or which demonstrates human intelligence. It includes all such activity, from the first manifestations of intelligence in an infant's behavioral repertoire to the adult intelligence as exemplified in logical operations.

There is no need to assert (nor do we imply) that thinking, even in its beginning stages, is restricted to human beings. On the contrary, an evolutionary viewpoint, which discovers continuity from the lower to the higher level of biological organisms, is desirable. Scientifically, such a view is preferable to either extreme: considering human intelligence as outside the realm of biological behavior or else freezing all behavior at a theoretical level applicable to rats in an experimental situation.

By the same token, thinking as human behavior is not something neatly separated from other human activities. It is as much a continuing part of our psychological life as the heart beat or the functioning of the nervous system is part of all physiological activity. When the psychologist studies thinking, he is really looking at psychological life as a whole from the aspect of intelligence. He will accordingly search for those behavioral samples which reveal more readily the processes of intellectual adaptation.

The above paragraph makes it abundantly clear that perception is not to be related to an infraintellectual activity, to be contrasted with conceptual and abstract thinking. If the bulk of our investigations center on "conceptual" behavior in the traditional sense, this is partly due to the fact that intellectual operations are more clearly inferred from conceptual tasks and nonverbal methods are more easily applied to them.

A "percept," as indicated above, is as much the result of an intellectual activity as a "concept." In both cases, the distinction between thinking activity and the result is highly artificial. As there is no concept without conceiving, there is no perception without perceiving. The same tendency which naïvely assumes concepts to be "in there," makes one too readily inclined to objectify perception as "out there." Both words, concept and percept, are abstract notions and should not be interpreted as representing accurately an objective state of affairs.

The view which assumes that perception is simply seeing what is out there, looks for the beginning of typical intelligent thinking in some abstractions which are performed on the perception or the image. Thus one neglects the organizing activity of the person who forms the percept and in so doing one fails to discover the roots of intelligent thinking in the most primitive and basic perceptual achievement. This also introduces a radical split between perceptual and conceptual thinking by calling the one concrete, the other abstract.

These points give an idea of the complexity of the task of clarification. If nothing else, they indicate that language is far from being a ready medium for clear and logical categories of living experience. The same linguistic structure is employed to state the three sentences: Tom has a coat. Tom has an illness. Tom has a thought. Do the three objects of the verb "has" represent similar categories of real life, having a similar degree of objective reality? If not, language is perhaps not entirely a faithful mirror of reality as it is known by the thinking person.

Perhaps it is a good thing that the presence of linguistically incompetent persons forces the behavioral scientist to study thinking without language. By this is implied not merely the necessity of employing nonverbal thinking tasks, but also a certain healthy skepticism with regard to linguistically determined notions.

In summary, it is proposed to understand by thinking any behavior specifically related to human intelligence. A concept or a percept is an abstract unit of thinking activity, in reality not distinguishable from thinking. A symbol, however, is objectively distinct from thinking, an observable event or at least an internal event which is experienced as distinct from the thinking person. A symbol is a product of thinking and it refers directly to thinking (concept). Within such a framework, language as a symbol system is objectively differentiated from thinking, and the question of the mutual relation between language and thinking can legitimately be raised.

It is planned to present first a general view of historical and contemporary positions regarding thinking and its relation to language. This is followed by the description of experimental work with deaf people and conclusions with regard to the thinking of the deaf together with some implications for contemporary theories on verbal mediation. A further chapter on thinking continues some points mentioned in this chapter and attempts to establish a theoretical view on the development of thinking. This view encourages the scientific empirical investigation of thinking and the specific questions raised in this project. It is a theoretical view not original with me but based on Piaget's observations, merely bringing into focus his view on matters germane to our purpose.

25

Chapter XIV is devoted to some educational implications and practical applications of the ideas expressed throughout the work. At the end there is, in answer to the questions raised in Chapter I, a concise statement of a number of theoretical positions to which this inquiry has led.

CHAPTER IV

Historical Perspective

In this chapter we wish to place the question concerning the relation of language and thinking in its historical context, and continue in Chapter V with a survey of contemporary opinions. This and the following chapter do not make any claim for completeness of coverage. Rather, the intent is to inquire into opinions on this problem from selected representatives of different schools of psychology and related disciplines. At times these scholars concerned themselves explicitly with thinking and language, more often, they left their suggested lines of opinion implicit in investigations of related problems.

Psychological theorizing—and we are speaking here of empirical and scientific psychology—on the relation of language and thinking has followed the prevailing philosophical opinions on this topic. Indeed, to do justice to the stated purpose of this chapter, one should start with philosophical ideas on this matter at a time when there was not only no empirical psychology but no empirical science. Such an undertaking is, however, beyond the scope of this book, nor is it necessary for the purpose at hand.

27

The history of deaf people provides an eloquent illustration of common opinion in past generations. The reader need only be reminded of what has been said in previous chapters about the deaf in the past and today, to realize that the so-called "intuitive" insight of the ordinary man concerning language and thinking was not only shared, but, argumentatively upheld by more sophisticated observers. Our opinion of the intelligence of the deaf has perhaps changed, but only with the condition that the word "mute" be dropped. As stated before, the deaf are now accepted as being possibly equal to the hearing in intelligence, but only insofar as they succeed in learning the language of the hearing. Common opinion about the interdependence of language and thinking has hardly changed. Let us now see whether the pronouncements or assumptions of scientists have developed in any new direction.

The second half of the nineteenth century saw the emergence of scientific psychology. What to us would seem an unbelievably small and perhaps trivial aspect of human life— measures of sensory responses, reaction time, rote learning— appeared to the German founders of the empirical science of psychology more than enough on which to base a new discipline. In fact, a breakthrough was made. For the first time, one did not speculate or write learned treatises on whether or not motoric reactions to sense stimuli were instantaneous, basing these judgments on tacit assumptions about the immateriality of psychological processes. One actually measured the reaction time and observed facts under controlled circumstances.

While Wundt and his followers stood on firm empirical ground in these matters, they were equally convinced that no empirical method could tell us much about thinking or reasoning. The reasons Wundt adduced for this belief centered around his private interpretation of "empirical method." Reading Wundt's attack on the German psychologists who a little later dared to study human thought, one is left with the distinct impression that Wundt was not so much concerned with psychology as an empirical science as he was with his philosophical assumptions about human nature. Despite his failure to recognize an empirical approach to thinking, Wundt must be credited with opening the way to the independent development of psychology as such.

Wundt limited the empirical method to artificially controlled observations of single conscious elements of behavior; this restriction limited the content matter of the new psychology as outlined above. Everything else in the human psyche—and Wundt, in contrast to "materialistic" philosophers, believed there was more in the human mind than sensations and their various combinations—belonged to a transcendental sphere, some innate spiritual principle of pure intellect which could not be studied by a *Naturwissenschaft* but was the domain of philosophical speculation or *Geisteswissenschaft*.

Human thought could only be studied, according to Wundt, in its verbal manifestation within a society. There was no doubt in his mind or those of his opponents, that the key to the study of thinking was the investigation of linguistic accomplishments.

Before crossing the ocean to see how an American contemporary of Wundt tackled the problem of thought and empirical method, we should note that Wundt's appeal to the study of literature as the means of investigating thought coincided with a flourishing empirical science of linguistics. In fact, study of the grammatical structure of past and present languages generated some startling discoveries of certain lawful changes in linguistic behavior. At that time these discoveries astonished those who were used to "physical" laws but were not inclined to conceive of "mental" phenomena as subject to equally binding laws. Uniformly accepted regular changes in phonemic and grammatical detail take place over generations and manifest the working of a "natural law." These lawful changes can be objectively and even quantitatively described to a much greater extent, for instance, than in any other historical discipline. Linguistics thus became the model and pride of the empirical method applied to a theoretical science. If we keep this in mind, it will help us understand why some contemporary psychologists, interested in thinking, have looked to linguistics as a guide and as a preferred approach. Wundt's reference to literature betrays his hope that the discovered laws of language may find a counterpart in to-be-discovered laws of thought.

William James, the American psychologist and philosopher, was of a different mettle altogether. He was not burdened with the Kantian philosophical heritage of transcendentalism or realism to the degree Wundt was. He felt no need to divide the mind into parts; one part open and another closed to empirical methods. Consequently he had no reason to limit empiricism to the content of conscious elements or to the special methodology of experimental control.

James, the psychologist, wrote freely on matters which would make many a psychologist blush. Thought, will, habit, morals, religion—all were treated by James as solidly as sensations and reaction-times. Like Wundt, he was still bound by the definition of psychology as the science of the conscious mind. It took Freud to put the unconscious on the scientific map and it took behaviorism to change the definition of psychology. But how different the consciousness of James looked compared to the neat clean sensory elements of Wundt!

Here we have James' famous "blooming, buzzing confusion," the stream of consciousness as he prefers to call it. Who could put exact order into this vital flow of intermingling, more or less conscious, states? Not James, for whom thinking was precisely this: an ever-expanding, indefinable, only partly conscious internal process of which we may become aware at certain "halting-places" but the essence of which rushes on beyond the pale of the introspective scientist.

The reader sees by this time that it makes little or no difference in what sort of mind-stuff, in what quality of imagery, his thinking goes on. The only images *intrinsically* important are the halting-places, the substantive conclusions, provisional or final, of the thought. Throughout all the rest of the stream, the feelings of relation are everything, and the terms related almost naught. These feelings of relation, these psychic overtones, halos, suffusions, or fringes about the terms, may be the same in very different systems of imagery (James, 1950, Vol. 1, p. 269).

James would have nothing to do with elements of thinking. The ephemeral halting-places in which thinking is supposed to take place were regarded by James as mental constructs of introspection, not something essential for the psychological investigator. Perhaps then Wundt was right when he asserted psychology should not attempt to study an individual's thinking process.

James' answer to this apparent dilemma is given in his pragmatic approach. The empirical scientist, he asserts, should not ask the question "What do I think in?" or "What are the elements that make up my thinking?" Rather he should address himself to the question "What is thinking for?" "What is the biological function of that which I can only report as 'it thinks?' " With this new phrasing of the question American functionalism was born. Who knows what would have happened to the psychology of thinking if James had been heeded in his remarks concerning the function of human thinking? James has been, in general, accepted as an adversary of the introspective, elementaristic method in psychology, but his general approach to the area of thinking was still too much tinged with philosophical considerations and not sufficiently supported by empirical observation to lead to a truly empirical investigation of thinking.

31

James does not fall back on verbal language to explain thinking or intelligence. Nor does he have kind words about mental images in connection with thinking. He sees no reason why a deaf person, that is, a person without the natural oral language of his society, should not be a perfectly intelligent being.

On the other hand, a deaf and dumb man can weave his tactile and visual images into a system of thought quite as effective and rational as that of a word-user. *The question whether thought is possible without language* has been a favorite topic of discussion among philosophers. Some interesting reminiscences of his childhood by Mr. Ballard, a deaf-mute instructor in the National College at Washington, show it to be perfectly possible (p. 266).

Unless I am mistaken this is the first time a scholar spoke of thinking, deafness, and language without implying that the presence or absence of language made a person's thinking better or worse.

Unfortunately, the term "functional" has a depreciative connotation, as if something which is useful is thereby less beautiful or less true. Of course, Americans did not really believe in this and the successors of James became "applied" psychologists (a much-abused value term) and invaded schools, hospitals, military services, industry, etc., and served a practical purpose. They were interested in education, emotional adjustment, and human efficiency and did not really care to study thinking for its own sake. Thus, the functional approach to the biological phenomenon of thinking was neglected so far as scientific psychology was concerned.

In the meantime, the "pure" school of psychological science continued, in the steps of Wundt, to look for the elements of consciousness. At the beginning of this century a group of German psychologists made a concerted effort to study human thinking. This was the famous school of German "thought psychology," against which the venerable founder of psychology in his old age thundered his censorial lightnings.

How did these investigators propose to study human thinking? A typical example will illustrate their method.

A person is presented with a series of cards on which are written simple tasks or commands such as: Part of House; Superordinate of Tailor; Give an Example of Musical Instrument. The person is to give a verbal response to each card and then report what he was conscious of while searching for the answer.

Two points become immediately obvious. First, these investigators were studying language as much as thinking. To ask for a superordinate of the word "tailor" requires linguistic mastery of the verbal instructions, including the word "superordinate" and the particular stimulus term. It further channelled thinking according to linguistic constraints insofar as a verbal reply is required. If our language had a collective term for professions concerned with the attire of persons—the tailor, the dressmaker, the hatter, the shoemaker, the furrier—or if it had a collective term for workers in cloth, different replies could be expected. We should not be surprised that the replies were influenced by language, since they are a part of language.

The second point has to do with method and aim. The aim was to report through introspection what the "halting-places" were which led to the verbal reply. We know what James thought of this procedure and are not surprised that unanimity was achieved only when a particular observer insisted upon finding what he was supposed to be seeking. Orthodox followers of Wundt insisted that there must be an internal image on which thinking is based. Included in the term "image" was internal language of some sort, the visually imagined written word, the heard word, and muscle movements of articulatory organs. Thus it could be said that thinking always took place "in" something.

33

The more daring and, it would seem, more objective psychologists of thinking submitted that an image or an internal palpable experience was not necessary for thinking. Actually different observers reported everything from muscle movements, kinesthetic sensations, states of tension, palpable awarenesses, visual images of varying degrees of clarity, auditory images of verbal or other events, internal sensations— to absolutely nothing. Thus arose around the time of the First World War the ill-fated "imageless thought controversy." Both sides were blocked by their assumption that thought can only be studied by discovering the elements of mental experience. Both were looking for "something" in which or by which we think.

Scholars on both sides of the Atlantic saw the futility of this argument and reacted accordingly. In Germany the *Gestalt* school attacked the elementaristic component of the old psychology and pointed out that what we report as ordinary perception certainly is not made up of a multitude of originally perceived sensory elements but strikes us as a whole. They emphasized that our organism imposes certain structures on the environment which originate in our innate or learned abilities. Although the investigations carried on by the *Gestalt* school were mainly concerned with perceptual tasks, the founder of the school, Wertheimer, left an unfinished manuscript on thinking which illustrates the approach to this problem.

The *Leitmotif* recurring in this writing is the term "restructuring" (*Umstruktur*) which refers to the new structure of a problematic situation that emerges once the key to its solution is found. The enlarged posthumous edition of Wertheimer's writings on thinking (1959) includes a short chapter of special interest for us since it deals with appraisal of the intelligence of young deaf children. Insofar as the author had an opportunity to relate language to intelligence, it is remarkable to find no indication that he considered the deaf children

34

less intelligent than others. His only concern was to devise tasks that would tell us something of the nonverbal child's intelligence. In general, then, *Gestalt* psychologists appeared to minimize the importance of language in thinking, but the reader should bear in mind that the contributions of the *Gestalt* school, while widely acceptable in the field of perception, were not in the mainstream of American psychology insofar as *thinking* was concerned.

That mainstream of psychological investigation was established after World War I in America with a resolute turning away from the search for the contents of consciousness. The German imageless thought controversy had shown the futility of the introspective method, and American pragmatism had opened the way for the application of psychological measurement to practical purposes without bothering at all about questions that smacked of speculative philosophy.

The battle cry of this new school was: Down with the mental, with consciousness, with all that cannot be pointed at or measured! Interest was centered only in what was outwardly observable, measurable, controllable. To the behaviorists, psychology as a science was based only on objective facts, not on subjectively changing reports of what is supposed to take place within the head. Here indeed was a revolt, not merely against method but against the very subject matter of psychology. Henceforth psychology was no longer to be defined in terms of human consciousness, but as an empirical science concerned with behavior.

However we may feel about the philosophical assumptions implied in the behaviorist approach, we must admit that some change of direction was desperately needed. It had become painfully clear that a direct investigation of consciousness could never establish psychology as a science independent of philosophy, because the very term consciousness was itself a philosophically tinged notion.

Behaviorism took the young science of American psychology by storm. The consequences were far-reaching and lasting. No longer was the emphasis on studying human consciousness. The accent now was on behavior, mainly in the form of learning. One dealt with objectively measurable change in a certain performance. Moreover, since strict experimental controls were desirable and human learning was obviously complex and multiple determined, the bulk of systematic learning experiments was performed on nonhuman organisms. This work was supported by theories to account for the behavioral results. Theories in turn influenced further experimental investigation and new theoretical explanations. Gradually theoretical notions became more complex, more mathematical and began to incorporate findings or theories from the field of neurophysiology.

If a visitor from Mars could read the literature of American experimental psychology during the second quarter of the twentieth century, he would certainly gain a peculiar picture of human life. He would gather that human beings had senses providing information about the outside world, that they were capable of discriminating sense-data and generalizing, that men could memorize and learn certain things by rote. Apart from a number of other possible inferences, human life as portrayed on these pages would seem meager indeed. He would find that human learning was similar to animal conditioning or training, and that logical reasoning was reduced to discrimination and generalization as exemplified in the concept formation of the monkey. While previous psychologists had sought the elements of human consciousness, the behaviorists no longer looked for the elements of behavior — human or otherwise. These were assumed to be necessarily stimulus and response. These investigators were merely interested in discovering conditions under which these elements became interconnected, so that each response would be determined by a pre-existing stimulus situation and each stimulus situation could be objectively described.

The tone of behavioristic theory was set by its founder, Watson, who proposed that what is called thinking may be nothing but subaudible speech. In other words, thinking is just silent language. What is notable about such a statement is not so much that it appeared to have been universally accepted—many will argue that Watson recognized it as an oversimplification—but rather, hardly anyone cared to oppose it. It was simply that human thinking as such was no longer of particular concern to American scientific psychologists.

Today the general atmosphere has changed somewhat. A number of scholars are now vitally interested in the development of thinking and language from birth to adulthood, in their mutual relation and the neurological apparatus at work. We shall survey the present scene under the term psycholinguistics since much, though not all, psychological activity concerning thinking can be brought under this heading. Before going on to these considerations, however, it is appropriate to turn to two nonpsychological trends which have influenced modern psychology and psycholinguistics in particular. Both trends emphasize language, one in the context of anthropology, the other as part of modern philosophical thought.

The writings of Benjamin Whorf (1956) in the period before World War II have greatly influenced today's interest in the relation between language and thinking. Whorf divided his concern equally between anthropology and linguistics. More exactly, he was the first to see some rather exciting anthropological implications in linguistic studies of societies with a different cultural tradition from our own. His own investigations along this line led him to the hypothesis that the language of a given society shapes the thinking of individual members of that society. He presented a variety of rather compelling illustrations showing that specific linguistic expressions determine to a great extent important aspects of behavior. Whorf's examples can be classed under three head-

37

ings: a) language as a substitute for thought; b) language as selectively emphasizing certain environmental stimuli; and c) language as constraining our mode of thinking.

Illustrations of the first point need hardly be given since the power of words is well known and recognized in advertising, politics, and ordinary social exchange. Whorf observes, for example, that around an industrial storage area marked "Gasoline Drums," employees take great care in fire prevention, while if the sign reads "Empty Gasoline Drums" (potentially much more dangerous on account of explosive vapor), little concern is shown for the danger of fire. Apparently the word "empty" is taken as synonymous for "null," "void," or "inert" and thus determines behavior in that situation.

It is, however, less clearly realized that these samples are not so much an illustration of linguistic influence on thinking as of an abdication of thinking in the presence of verbal stimuli. No doubt much verbal behavior proceeds at a fairly habitual, quasi-automatic level. Hence it would seem important not to identify just any verbal behavior with thinking behavior. The latter term might rather be reserved for activities internally controlled by principles which are themselves the product of thinking; they are not merely controlled by internalized verbal habits.

The second group of examples given by Whorf concerns the fact that we are more likely to pay attention to things or events in our environment as the natural language records them. He found that other societies than ours divide the color continuum differently and perceive it accordingly. Likewise in certain areas of the world, weather conditions and actions are differently understood and described, according to the significance they have for individuals in that particular environment. Whorf's observations along this line, while striking and interesting, directly concern only a narrow spectrum of thinking activity in the area of perception and recognition.

Moreover, experimenters who attempted to investigate the dependence of perceptual activity on the social language have found that with some short term training observed differences between linguistic groups could be readily overcome, an indication that one does not deal here with a deep seated basic difference in perception. Furthermore, the question should legitimately be raised whether it is language influencing behavior in these instances or the needs and practices of the given society dictating both behavior and language.

It is then only in the third group that Whorfian linguistic relativity, interpreted in the sense of a strict dependence of thinking upon language, can hope to find empirical support. Whorf points out, for instance, that our European-derived notion of time as manifested in language is quite different from linguistic expressions related to time in some American Indian societies. He suggests that language contributes heavily toward our metaphysical structure in which we view time in a clock-like fashion as an even flowing change from future to present to past—a notion quite foreign and presumably incomprehensible to certain Indian societies. Related to our concept of time, Whorf sees our European drive toward perfection, competition, and intellectual exploration. Such subtle and all-pervasive influences, whether or not they are primarily carried by the natural language, are difficult to put to an empirical test. Moreover, they seem to encompass much more than what we would term thinking in the present context. For that reason we related this third group of behavioral events to "mode of thinking." Such instances of supposed linguistic determinism can be classified under general cultural influences. These influences are obviously strong and bound to be present in thinking, in language, and in any other behavior.

The second influence on the contemporary psychology of thinking and language is related to the modern philosopher's preoccupation with language. Positivism in the latter part of the 19th century was part of the general philosophical atmosphere contributing to the emergence of scientific psychology. In connection with scientific knowledge, philosophers stressed the importance of testable facts, either immediately observed or derived in strictly logical fashion. As a natural by-product of the philosopher's concern for a valid basis of his verbal pronouncement, there emerged a lively concern for the verbal language constantly employed by philosophers and scientists. This concern is as much alive today as when it first began.

From this preoccupation with language one may single out for special attention the term "operational definition," which since the 1930's has become a standard phrase in psychological writings. The term relates to the need for clarifying the significance of words which are used in scientific reporting. When I mention an experiment employing "twenty thirty-to-forty-year-old subjects each of high and low anxiety," I must explain as unambiguously as possible what I mean by those words. Numbers and chronological age are fairly clear, but the word "anxiety" is definitely not uniformly understood by everyone. An operational definition reduces this ambiguity to a minimum by stating the observable operations performed for classifying the subjects in one of the two groups. Such an operation may be the total score on a questionnaire designed to measure anxiety, or it may be a number of items checked on a list of behavioral characteristics of anxiety, or perhaps it is some physiological measurement supposedly related to anxiety.

A defining procedure of this kind is of course most desirable if in practice it does not limit the initiative of the scientist. An operational definition is somewhat like the concept of limited liability insofar as the scientist may feel free from any responsibility concerning the appropriateness of his operation and from the necessity of probing more deeply into the thing that is supposed to be measured. After using a word like "intelligence" a thousand times and defining it operationally as a score on a certain standard test, or after speaking of "criterion of attainment" of a concept as a given number of errorless trials, it is easy to slip into the erroneous assumption that now we know a great deal about intelligence or concept attainment.

Operational definitions should be at most temporary scaffoldings in scientific endeavors, not stones with which a lasting structure may be built. They were intended to give significance to words, not merely to denote an operation whose significance is of little concern to the scientist and may be of minimal substance for the science itself. The danger of having trivial or invalid operations in place of potentially ambiguous words, is particularly critical because operational definitions have a respectable scientific flavor common words do not enjoy. In summary, there can be no doubt that a falsely placed reliance on operational definitions has had an inhibiting influence on the development of a psychological science of thinking.

A final section is in order about the field of study which deals directly with word meanings: the science of signs (or semiotic) which developed in the wake of growing concern in philosophical circles about the nature and use of symbols, particularly as exemplified in natural verbal language. Scholars in this field make more or less explicit statements about the close relation of language and thinking and frequently seem to claim that a correct use of verbal symbols is a guarantee of valid thinking.

Take a word like "meaning" and think of the many different ways in which it can be employed in ordinary conversation. Yet "meaning" appears to be one, if not *the,* main attribute of verbal signs. Morris (1946) proposes a distinction in connection with the meaning of signs which is followed in this book. Any verbal sign or symbol "means" something, Morris suggests (p. 18), but not every symbol "denotes" something. The term denotation is restricted to the relation of symbol to an objective instance. The term signification is used concerning the relation of the symbol to its thinking user. Without

41

signification, there would be no symbol and in signification is found a symbol's direct reference or meaning. Yet to the positivist scientist, denotation is of paramount importance. Denotation relates the symbol, or perhaps better, the symbol-user, to objective reality. Any objective event that exemplifies a symbol is said to denote it.

Denotation is related to operational definition. The word "chair" signifies a specific concept and denotes a particular piece of furniture which may exist in various shapes and types. The utterance "The ice cream cone supports the weight of the skyscraper" is a comprehensible statement, as far as signification goes, but no objective event is likely to be observed which can be said to denote this utterance.

Langer (1964, pp. 63–64) agrees in part with the above terminology and shows that denotation is always a two-step relation, that is, the relation of a symbol to an instance through a person's conception. "In denotation which is the simplest kind of symbol-function, there have to be four [essential terms]: subject, symbol, conception and object." But Langer restricts the term "signification" to nonsymbolic signs and prefers the term "connotation" for the direct relation of a symbol to its concept. It should be noted that here the word "connotation" is used in the logical sense as just indicated and not in the more colloquial sense of a suggestive significance or association apart from a term's explicitly recognized meaning. For Langer as for Morris, the mediate reference of a symbol to the physical object is its denotation.

Langer submits—as good "functional" thinking—that the meaning of a term can be found only in its function and that the function of a sign "rests on a pattern, in which the term itself holds the key-position." In distinction from *symbol*-meaning, *signal*-meaning requires only three terms: subject, signal, and object. Langer reserves for the relation signal-object the term signification. She continues: "The radical difference between sign-meaning and symbol-meaning can

42

therefore be logically exhibited, for it rests on a difference of patterns, it is strictly a different function."

With this position, Langer follows through with a suggested difference between symbolic and nonsymbolic signs, or "signals" as Morris calls them. Morris refers to this distinction as "basic in the literature of semiotic" (p. 23). He lists as characteristics of symbols that they are produced by the organism and stand for other signs. But as "a symbol is ultimately a substitute for signal" (p. 25), Morris sees no need, as does Langer, to distinguish between symbol-meaning or signal-meaning. Consequently, though the distinction between symbol and signal is called basic, Morris in practice follows the behavioristic trend by not stressing any basic difference between symbol and signal in function and behavior.

This short review of past positions is a prelude to an equally brief sketch of contemporary views. While psychologists, philosophers, and linguists attempt in their own way to comprehend the functioning of the verbal human organism, all appear to agree that verbal behavior and thinking behavior are related. One can recognize that several questions pertaining to the language-thinking relation have been asked and left unanswered. It is equally noteworthy that many of the crucial questions are interrelated: "Do signs differ from symbols?" seems but another way of asking: "Does signal-knowledge differ from symbol-knowledge?" And this in turn is similar to the question: "Is thinking a different kind of activity than sensory-motor behavior?" Without waiting for answers to these questions, many scholars look to *language* as the royal road to the explanation of what is characteristically *human behavior*. This assumed close relation between human thinking and language is typified in the term: "psycholinguistics," the title of Chapter V.

Contemporary Psycholinguistics

The section of our survey concerned with contemporary positions on the relation of thinking and language falls to a large extent into that area of scientific psychology which deals with linguistic behavior. Significantly, modern psychology is somewhat more willing to accept a psychology of language than of thinking. The term "psycholinguistics" was coined during the 1950's to express the twin origin of this new branch of scientific psychology from linguistics on the one hand and psychology on the other.

The dominant school of behaviorism, we have noted, tended to shy away from verbal behavior together with other "mental" terms, such as thinking, knowing, or consciousness. However, beginning around 1930, psychology became increasingly aware of the fact that it, like any other science, constantly used language in articulating, expressing, and communicating its findings. Under the impact of logical positivism and semantics, psychologists paid closer attention to the verbal medium in which their statements were couched. They learned to differentiate observable facts from verbal inferences made on the basis of facts and they explicitly classed some inferences as hypothetical constructs. With these precautions it became clear even to the most "hard-headed" psychologists that linguistic behavior could be studied as an observable, reliable event in its own right.

In the meantime, linguists had successfully employed empirical methods to study verbal behavior and psychologists were prepared and even eager to work with them in an area they had neglected but which seemed to fall within the range of psychological investigation. From a historical point of view, acceptance of psycholinguistics as a legitimate branch of scientific psychology is significant, if for no other reason than that it marks a new beginning of systematic psychological study of linguistic behavior and all it entails.

In its present state psycholinguistics is not and perhaps never will be a unified, clearly definable specialty of psychology. The very term language is so broad that no aspect of human behavior can be said to be outside its influence. To present the topic of psycholinguistics in an orderly fashion, six major approaches or areas are delineated in the following section with some brief mention of pertinent research. It is not proposed that we go into a detailed description of individual positions, and the specific selection of approaches or the names may appear arbitrary. The purpose of this chapter is to present a brief contemporary overview, particularly to those readers less familiar with current psychological literature.

Emphasis will be on the language-thinking relation as shown in the writings of contemporary behavioral scientists. The six approaches may be said to differ in the way in which they regard language. They are: 1. normative; 2. material; 3. mediating; 4. linguistic; 5. pathological; and 6. "neo-behavioral."

1. In the *normative* approach, the investigator is primarily concerned with the end product, namely, the finished word or sentence, either spoken or, more frequently, written. He uses these raw data to gather facts and generate laws about such

matters as word frequency or probability of certain letter or word combinations. He collects developmental norms about word usage and attempts to test verbal output by following grammatical usage or by creating new *ad hoc* linguistic categories.

Under this heading can be placed word association norms that have been established for various populations and age groups. Another characteristic example is the experimental work that has been done with words ranging in letter order from an order closely approaching the natural order of English to nonsense words structurally or by association minimally related to English. Similar experiments have been reported on the order of words within a sentence.

In general, workers using this approach keep close to factual data and their implications do not generalize into the area of thinking.

2. In this section could be grouped those studies in which verbal behavior is observed under experimental conditions. However, language is considered merely as the *material* being learned. In this sense the approach to language is here termed *material* although, paradoxically, it is referred to in psychological literature as "verbal learning."

Studies of rote learning which frequently employ nonsense words are pertinent. The aim is to discover lawful influences of certain variables, e.g., training conditions, similarity of material, frequency of exposure, and temporal factors, on final performance. In general, investigators attempt to study verbal behavior under conditions which make it maximally similar to a relatively simple response of a lower organism. After divesting language of certain characteristics (spontaneity, significance, communication, and natural and informal learning) which do not fit easily into the behavioristic experimental paradigm, investigators found that verbal behavior follows laws similar to those found in lower animals.

This view has become popular through Skinner's (1957)

exposition of verbal behavior. The keyword in Skinner's position is the term reinforcement. He, and those of his persuasion, claim that reinforcement determines linguistic as well as other behavior. Consequently the conditions for its experimental control and investigation are present. Since by definition any behavior that takes place has been reinforced, one can assert that in most human situations the term reinforcement does not explain much unless reinforcing conditions can be formally specified. An illustration should clarify these considerations.

Skinner is concerned with identifying in summary fashion some of the events commonly associated with verbal behavior. Thus he holds that the baby in his early babbling makes all the sounds known to the languages of mankind, but through selective reinforcement and extinction he comes to speak in the sounds of his native tongue. Babies living in England learn to speak English, while those born in China learn to speak Chinese. More specifically, a child tends to imitate the words he hears and thus learns to bring about a change in the environment and to satisfy a need by verbal behavior. Or he wins approval by giving a verbal name in the presence of a given stimulus event. These situations illustrate, according to Skinner, ways in which children learn a verbal response. In each situation there is said to be present a reinforcing factor which controls the child's response. The reinforcing conditions are satisfaction of some need or, if no specific need condition can be observed, as is commonly the case, a general need for social approval is postulated.

The question of "meaning" does not really enter into the scheme and reinforcement is said to work in language as in any other kind of behavior. While it is comparatively easy to state the general conditions responsible for a child's learning one specific language rather than another, it is much less obvious what the reinforcing conditions are that determine the utterance of a simple sentence like "I went to my friend's house." If reinforcement as a theoretical construct plays a determining role in the production of verbal responses, it would seem that the scientist should point them out before the response is made rather than be satisfied with a general classification of possible reinforcers that are specified after the response is observed.

As most deaf children do not succeed in learning language despite constant training and reinforcement over a period of ten years and longer, we might justifiably wonder whether reinforcement is really the key to language learning. If the reinforcing conditions include some specific external and possibly internal conditions which are not present in deaf children, these conditions should be explicitly stated and formally related to language learning. As long as reinforcement is proposed to be *the* controlling variable, failure to learn language can only be imputed to the wrong kind of reinforcers or to the inappropriate rate or quantity of reinforcement. In this view the sheer number or frequency of exposure to correct reinforcing conditions can explain mastery of language for the hearing. As to thinking and its relation to language, the Skinnerian approach is frankly not applicable.

3. Other scientists do not adhere so strictly to merely outward events as do those of the Skinnerian school. They are prepared to admit some unobservable responses of a physiological or psychological nature as *mediating* in a lawful manner between outward observable events. Some internal events are assumed to intervene between external events, hence the term "intervening variables."

These scientists are still convinced that verbal behavior can be explained in terms of a behavioristic stimulus-response model. But they do admit that the simple model of Skinner should be enlarged to explain such specific behavior as comprehension of an ordinary sentence.

For example, we may hear the spoken words: "Please bring me a pencil from the upper right drawer of the desk." We observe the corresponding overt action following this request. Obviously some immediately unobservable past event on the part of the listener together with the verbal demand must have been responsible for the appropriate reaction since there is no directly given connection between the verbal demand and the outward action. In ordinary language we would say the listener understood the meaning of the sentence and acted accordingly. For the psychologist, however, "meaning" is the riddle to be unraveled.

Osgood (1953) assumes that meaning is an internal part-response to an outward event, this part-response being present both in the verbal and in the real denoted situation. In perceiving a cup we make perhaps some internal movements within the eye or the muscles of the hand. Learning the meaning of the sound-sequence "C–U–P" consists, according to Osgood, of associating the sounds with some internal movements, present in the perception of a real cup. In this way the spoken word "cup" is reacted or responded to by the organism as if it were the visually perceived object. The internal response can in turn become an internal stimulus and elicit another internal or external response.

Comprehension of language is thus said to be mediated by internal, not readily observable, responses. These mediating responses fit into a simple conditioning paradigm. Someone has observed that the failure of subhuman organisms to learn language should be rather embarrassing to such an explanation since generally it is easier to condition a behavioral response in lower organisms than in humans.

Following Osgood's lead, other scholars more directly interested in general learning than in learning of language found that an internal verbal intervening response could conveniently be postulated in types of learning that do not readily fall into a simple stimulus-response paradigm. A great number of investigations now center around the topic of verbal mediation.

Verbal mediation is most easily pictured as covert or inner

language of which a person need not necessarily be aware. An experiment demonstrating such mediation may start with training children to find a reward consistently under a black box and never under a white box. These boxes may vary inconsistently in form, but form is an irrelevant dimension for this task. After succeeding on this task, the reward is reversed, that is, white is now consistently reinforced instead of black. Such a "reversal shift" is usually easier for children from age six on than a "nonreversal shift" in which the previously irrelevant dimension of form is reinforced and color becomes the irrelevant dimension. For younger children and subhuman organisms, a nonreversal is usually found to be easier than a reversal shift. According to Kendler and Kendler (1959), the explanation of the difference in behavior between humans over age six and younger children or animals may lie in the fact that older humans form a mediating verbal response to the dimension and hence find it easier to shift within that dimension than to a new dimension.

Here for the first time is an example of linking language and thinking within a stimulus-response framework so that conceptual thinking could be treated in a behavioral paradigm of stimulus and response with the mediating help of an internal linguistic response. What is critical for our discussion is the fact that a verbal mediating response is postulated. In ordinary language we would say that the person has learned to react to a specific aspect of a stimulus rather than to the global stimulus as a whole, i.e., the person *abstracts* from form and attends primarily to the concept of color.

Suddenly it appeared that the whole area of thinking, formerly given short shrift by experimental psychologists, could be incorporated into a theoretical framework of verbal mediation. The most ambitious undertaking in this connection is undoubtedly the work by Staats and Staats (1963) which attempts to build the entire structure of logical reasoning, social and motivational behavior on the theoretical blend of internal verbal mediation and Skinnerian control of behavior.

The authors are straightforward in their explanation. They employ, in addition to the mediating verbal response or stimulus, some internal form of generalization which enables a person to generalize a verbal rule. Accordingly, (pp. 219 ff) the child learns mathematics when he learns to make verbal responses like "two and two equals four," "two and three equals five," "three minus two equals one." These responses are learned through reinforcement. Then they become internalized and with sufficient repetition and examples the child forms such internal verbal generalizations as: "The elements in an addition problem can be interchanged without changing the sum," or, "The remainder plus the subtrahend equals the minuend." These verbal rules are then assumed to control correct mathematical behavior and insofar as they are reinforced by society and practical results such behavior is indefinitely maintained.

Social rules are learned in a similar manner. Even sexual behavior is said to be largely controlled by internal verbal responses learned during the period of growth. Heterosexual attachment is considered largely a matter of having heard and learned the correct verbal rule (pp. 398 ff). In a similar verbal manner, differences in sexual mores among different social classes may be explained.

These developments are most pertinent to the theme and purpose of our book. From postulating a mediating variable in human language learning, from linking thinking to internal linguistic responses, the entire repertoire of human behavior is built up on the basis of verbal mediation; moreover, mediation is assumed to be a type of behavior of which subhuman organisms are quite capable. There are thus three major assumptions on which this reasoning is based. These assumptions can be stated as follows: Thinking is reduced to language; language is reduced to a mediating response; and the mediating response to conditioning.

51

4. The *linguistic* approach in contemporary psycholinguistics is at the base of much psychological work on the topic of language and thinking, insofar as psychologists adopt models and theoretical positions from linguists. The primary focus of linguists is language in the sense of a finished corpus of utterances rather than linguistic behavior and its relation to nonlinguistic aspects of the psychological situation.

Nevertheless, it was Chomsky's insight that a formal meaningful description of language must be viable in behavior and must provide a valid model for the behavioral study of language. He pointed out two deficiencies of ordinary descriptive linguistics. First, it is actually incomplete and assumes as a prerequisite an intuitive grasp of language, and second, it is largely based on *ad hoc* constructs and is not vitally or formally related to linguistic universals. Chomsky (1962) made the rather bold assertion that a formal model of language should provide rules and principles by which any correct utterance of a particular language could be generated and he further hypothesized that such a generative model may well coincide with what implicitly takes place in a person competent in a language.

With this suggestion Chomsky places himself on the side of those who seek a model of thinking not based on language. Necessarily, there is one body of knowledge we do not acquire by means of language and that is competence in natural language, achieved by practically all human beings by the age of four.

For psychologists, perhaps the most pertinent of Chomsky's ideas relates to his theory on levels of structure and transformational rules. While other linguists attacked an utterance such as: "How was the orchestra led by the conductor?" by directly analyzing the end product, Chomsky thinks of the rules which generated this utterance. Surely the sentence: "In which way did the conductor lead the orchestra?" or even: "The conductor leads the orchestra" is much closer to the original sentence than the following, which yet consists of similar syntactical units: "How was the dinner prepared by the cook?"

Linguists in the past, not unlike present-day psychologists, strove valiantly to keep the meaning aspect out of linguistics and in so doing they found it hard to recognize formally the closeness of sentences with similar meaning while concentrating on similarities in finished syntactical structures. Chomsky now proposes the existence of deep structures underlying the manifest or surface structures. Thus two sentences with very different surface structures may yet be generated from identical or similar deep structures. And in turn two similar surface structures may be the product of quite different deep structures. Between the deep and the surface structure, a number of obligatory and optional transformational rules operate. Chomsky proposes that it is the linguist's task to discover the generating rules, a task which should clarify the meaning of linguistic competence.

These and other ideas are now being tested by psychologists whose primary aim is to observe linguistic behavior, often in a developmental framework. The result is the appearance of a number of systematic studies of language of a type quite different from what has gone before. There are hopeful signs that this will develop into a full blown psychology of language.

Will this development enrich our psychological understanding of thinking? Not in a direct manner, I believe, since the movement is directed to linguistic skill. It could even hinder our search for formal constructs of thinking if we do not keep firmly to the important distinction between language as one model of thinking and language as the means of thinking.

5. The *pathological* approach in psycholinguistics should be given at least passing mention since studies dealing with the deaf may be classed in this division. However, this section is particularly concerned with adult persons who through injury

53

to the nervous system suffer various losses in linguistic skills. A history of scholarly opinions on aphasia proves most enlightening concerning the underlying and frequently unanalyzed assumptions about linguistic and thinking behavior.

These assumptions have changed from the "diagram makers" of the second half of the 19th century—neurologists who thought in terms of a one-to-one correspondence between word, image and cerebral location—to the notions of Jackson and Head who considered aphasia in terms of loss of propositional language, or of Goldstein who originated the distinction of concrete vs. abstract attitude. Head's (1926) observations influenced the British psychology of thinking considerably. Generally, experts have not made impressive progress since the days of Head. The question remains open whether aphasia should be considered a *specific* linguistic deficiency or a *general* cognitive defect to which verbal behavior is most sensitive. Moreover, none of the suggested divisions or types of aphasia are formal, in the sense of fitting into a compelling theoretical schema, or distinct without much overlapping and blurring of boundaries.

This is not the place for a detailed discussion on various past or present opinions, there is however, sufficient general agreement and impressive evidence concerning the fact that severe and at times total deficiency in linguistic behavior can be present without an equally severe general deficit in thinking. While the predominance of the linguistic failure is apparent and gives the syndrome its name, the concomitant loss in intellectual functioning is open to questions and speculations. Thus, the objective condition of aphasia is something which any theory on thinking or language must eventually be tested against.

Verbal deficiency may of course be associated with other circumstances, such as lack of hearing, i.e., deafness, lack of general intellectual ability (low IQ), or emotional disturbance. Its specific form may vary from complete or partial absence of language comprehension to the inability to express oneself orally. It is worth noting that in educational circles the term "psycholinguistic deficiency" may comprise a variety of disparate conditions, e.g., difficulties in learning to read or write, or delayed and impaired speech.

6. The trend in some of the foregoing psychological approaches was to clarify questions about the use and function of language in terms of very general behavioral characteristics without considering linguistic behavior as exemplifying any special competence, but in the *neo-behavioral* approach the respective roles of language and behavior tend to be reversed. The investigator's aim is to enlarge our knowledge of human behavior by studying linguistic activity, that is recognized as different from behavior that is explainable in terms of conditioning. Investigators using this approach appear to have in common a willingness, vis-à-vis language and thinking, not merely to expand the stimulus-response model into longer chains but to use a theoretical approach beyond or apart from strict behaviorism. In short, they attribute to linguistic and thinking behavior characteristics for which the conditioning model appears insufficient. They do not by any means repudiate the main objectives of the behavioral approach, namely, to observe psychological phenomena in a maximally objective fashion, to employ operationally definable variables and to search for suitable empirical methods to probe into thinking and language behavior.

With emphasis on the language-thinking relation, contributions in this area can be grouped into four divisions, with one or more representatives in each division according to a geographical pattern. First, we shall consider the British school, as exemplified in the writings of Bartlett and Humphrey; then contributions from the United States, represented by Mowrer and by Bruner; third, the Russian school of the second signal system with Vygotsky and Luria; and finally, the organismic-developmental approach of Werner with roots in the German *Gestalt* psychology.

Britain. The English tradition is fairly represented by the work of Bartlett who published a volume on *Remembering* in 1932 and a second volume on *Thinking* in 1958. One is immediately impressed by the realistic approach so typical of the English empirical tradition. The author shies away from too great involvement in theoretical constructs or what may be called rigid "experimentology" by which the observed responses may lose "just that special character which initially made them the objects" of a psychologist's study (Bartlett, 1932, p. 6). At the same time he is sufficiently sophisticated not to fall prey to philosophical naïveté. He can spot unanalyzed assumptions, whether they come in the guise of philosophical or scientific conventions.

Ogden and Richards (1956, p. 82) state in the passage from which the title quotation was taken that "we can only discover the *how* of referents, not the *what*"; and that "this doctrine needs to be reaffirmed whenever the metaphysician intervenes, whether he comes as a *materialist,* spiritualist, dualist, realist or with any other answer to an impossible question" George Humphrey (1963, p. 228) also, in his historical work on thinking concludes that the problem of "meaning" has been beclouded by asking the wrong questions, whether in connection with speech or with concepts. In both cases, he suggests the reference function is simply a problem of learning, not a unique problem of meaning.

With such a general view, which can appear oversimplified to some, there is at least the assurance of keeping interest open to real life situations. Bartlett makes full use of this advantage. He turns resolutely to investigate thinking in its functions as it really occurs and considers it as an activity or a high level skill. When he does theorize, he does not ask in what or by what means we think, but the function thinking serves or expresses. He says already in connection with perceiving (1932, p. 193) that it is a function of (a) "a sensory pattern which has a physiological basis" and (b) "a psychological orientation or attitude which cannot be expressed in terms of any local bodily responding mechanism." In his more recent book (1958, p. 44), Bartlett states that the results of his studies afford no justification for the belief that abstraction and generalization comes about automatically by accumulation of particular instances. He appears to be in full agreement with Humphrey (1963) that motoric components, images or verbal language, may accompany but can never explain thinking. The fact that one has learned to attach a word to all kinds of instances without taking into account its singularity is what makes a word a general term, not the stating of a name.

It is curious that one theoretical construct related to thinking, which Bartlett employed extensively in his earlier book, is not made use of or even mentioned in the latter work. This is the term "schema" which Bartlett borrowed from Head, the neurologist. Head (1926) understood schema to be an internal postural pattern that implicitly guided motoric behavior similar to a norm or standard against which the central nervous system could compare subsequent postural positions. Bartlett (1932, pp. 201 ff) widened the meaning of the term schema and partly divested it of its neurological significance. He referred to schema as an internal organization of past reactions or experiences on the part of a person, an internal reconstruction or setting which rendered a specific adaptive reaction possible. This was the manner in which Bartlett attempted to conceptualize the active preparation with which the human organism seemed to respond to any present situation, whether in perceiving, in remembering, or thinking. Bartlett speculates only so far as to suggest that thinking and the use of language are closely connected and occur "biologically subsequent to the image-forming process . . . when a way has been found of breaking up the 'massed' influence of past stimuli and situa-

57

tions. . . ." The closest he comes to defining the specific biological function of thinking is: "The capacity of an organism to turn round upon its own schemata and to construct them afresh."

The notion of schema in its neurological aspect has in later years found some dramatic support by the discovery of the functioning of the nonspecific reticular formation within the central nervous system. This had led to increasingly neurologic speculations within psychology about the organismic happenings during perception, thinking, and speaking. On the other hand, Werner and Piaget have been using the term schema to denote something closely akin to Bartlett's notion, an internal organization to which an external event in actual behavior is assimilated. While their English colleague confined his observations to the adult person, Piaget and Werner spoke of schema within a developmental view of the growing child. Their views will be discussed in greater detail in Chapter XIII.

United States. For obvious reasons contemporary psychology could not be satisfied with this uncomplicated common sense description of thinking and language. With its heavy theoretically tinged stimulus-response legacy of behaviorism North American psychology was bound to continue in the direction of looking for hypothetical constructs that would explain thinking even when it was prepared to admit that more than a quantitative modification of the behavioristic stimulus-response model may be required.

Mowrer is perhaps the first American behaviorist to recognize the need for a distinction between signal and symbol. Mowrer's concern is language behavior and he observes that the sign behavior of animals is basically different from the sign behavior of humans. "Animals, it seems, are often extremely well equipped for the detection of remote and subtle stimuli and for learning, through conditioning, to attach special meanings to them. But they are much less well prepared

58

or disposed themselves to *make* stimuli that may have sign, or signaling, value" (1960, p. 125).

For Mowrer a symbol is a self-produced sign not necessarily associated with an inner need state. "When animals have no immediate 'practical' need for an object, they likewise have no interest in a sign thereof—and thus fall short of symbolic behavior" (p. 159).

Mowrer concludes that linguistic behavior manifests the presence of certain capacities which lower organisms do not possess and cannot be reduced to sign-learning.

Monkeys and apes have hands quite as good as our own; and their oral and vocal equipment seems completely adequate for speech. Why have *they* not developed linguistically, beyond the few stereotyped sounds previously discussed? Here one can only surmise that the remarkable mutation with respect to the "speech centers" of the brain which manifestly took place in the evolutionary line from which man has descended did not occur in these species (p. 129).

Implying a distinction between linguistic and intellectual skill on which he does not enlarge, Mowrer approvingly cites Dollard and Miller who point out that a parrot can learn to imitate words but cannot become a great thinker. In spite of these concessions to the particular role of human language, Mowrer proposes that the phenomenon of human thinking can be generally analyzed in terms of principles which have been demonstrated to hold in connection with experimental learning in less complex organisms.

Bruner's views on the relation of thinking and language are perhaps most succinctly outlined in an address to the American Psychological Association on stages in cognitive development. In this paper Bruner (1964) is concerned with the means or instrumentalities which make a human organism capable of intellectual growth. He describes these instrumentalities as modes of internal representation and calls them enactive, iconic, and symbolic representation in the developmental order

59

in which they become manifest in the growing child. Enactive relates to motoric response patterns, iconic to perceptual imagery, and symbolic to internalized language as a vehicle for organizing experience.

Like Mowrer, Bruner believes that symbolic functioning is a unique set of powers for internal control of behavior as distinguished from external stimuli or stimulus substitutes which control sub-human behavior. He goes further than Mowrer in identifying the specific role of language in mature thinking. This role is twofold, language not only represents experience but transforms it according to its own transformational rules. "Once the child has succeeded in internalizing language as a cognitive instrument, it becomes possible for him to represent and systematically transform the regularities of experience with far greater flexibility and power than before."

Borrowing some experiments from Piaget's laboratory, Bruner describes intellectual development as a function of the representative media. To succeed in Piaget's conservation problems (tasks that will be employed and described in detail in Chapter IX), the child must, according to Bruner, employ some internalized verbal formula that shields him from the pull of the perceptual appearance.

Even though Bruner may not go so far as to identify mature thinking with verbal language, he comes close to it by speaking of internalized speech as a prerequisite for logical thinking and linking the transformation of reality which occurs in thinking with specific linguistic transformational rules. The notion of the internalization of speech crops up in other writers too and its exact denotation is frequently kept vague so that it eludes a clear understanding. By referring to Vygotsky's theories on language and thinking, Bruner seems to take a stand on inner speech along with Soviet psychology. The next section summarizes this school with particular emphasis on the question of inner language.

60

Russia. It is rather remarkable that Russian psychology has never indulged in the kind of desperate effort that characterized American behaviorism to reduce human behavior to such a level that it can be discussed indiscriminately in terms applicable either to rats or to humans. Pavlov, it is said, was rather amused when he heard that American psychologists were applying his classical conditioning model of dogs to humans. Thus in Soviet Russia, with its dominant Marxist philosophy, experimental psychologists unhesitatingly regarded man's capacities as superior to and qualitatively different from those of lower animals.

Many psychologists in America who were concerned with the thinking capacities of humans found that a reductionistic behavior model could not do justice to the phenomenon of thinking. Likewise, developmental psychologists could not help noticing that children's growth was in terms of cognitive systems of increasing complexity and structural differentiation which could not readily be explained in behavioristic terms. These psychologists were delighted to find allies in the unexpected quarter of Soviet psychology.

A summary of the Soviet position on thinking and language starts with Pavlov's conditioning paradigm which characterizes animal behavior. Conditioning is based on need and association of a new stimulus with an original stimulus which satisfies the need. Pavlov employed this conditioning model to observe learned behavior in animals and to make inferences about the workings of the underlying nervous system. In humans, Pavlov observed that this so-called first signal system was not of primary importance; human behavior seemed to him controlled by a different system of signals, which are not exterior and do not satisfy an organic need. Pavlov suggested that language may well be at the root of this second signal system but made no detailed study of this hypothesis.

Vygotsky (1962) followed this suggestion by a close observation of the development of speech in children and by a study of the function of language and thinking in human and lower animals. The latter consideration led him to see speech and thought as serving different functions and as not correlated in subhumans. However, in humans, the development of these two functions crosses at a certain age and becomes intertwined, eventuating in the verbal and meaningful word of the mature person. Luria, as an exponent of Vygotsky's view, puts it in this form, referring to the overt speech which frequently accompanies purposeful action in children and continues as seemingly repetitious verbalization.

These verbal repetitions are preserved for some time, but in the six to seven year old child they die away and vanish. What is characteristic here is the fact that, with the appearance of verbal formulations—in other words with inclusion of the child's own speech in his orientation to the signals presented—the very process of elaboration of new connections changes. Connections which were previously elaborated gradually, which needed permanent reinforcement and were extinguished when it was removed, begin now to be elaborated quickly, sometimes "on the spot," become stably reinforced, cease to be in need of permanent reinforcement and begin to show those features of "self regulation" which Pavlov regarded as the essential peculiarity of human higher nervous activity . . . (Luria and Yudovich, 1959, p. 20).

Vygotsky suggests that children's early speech mirrors the phylogenetic development. Their speech serves mainly as a signal function, i.e., to express an internal state of emotional or organic need, and their thinking, described above as "the elaboration of new connections," proceeds according to patterns which have nothing to do with language. There comes a point, however, in the child's development, when he discovers the "symbolic" function of words and employs speech in the service of thinking. First this is done externally, i.e., the child uses spoken language both to communicate and to think. Finally, speech structures, mastered by the child through contact with the social environment, are internalized and with further development become the basic structures of human thinking.

For Vygotsky, inner and external speech stand for two radically different functions of language, the one serving the ego in thinking, the other in social communication. Inner speech stands between the word and the "pure" thought. It is that aspect of the thinking function which has come under the influence of language or again it is that aspect of the speech function which serves thinking.

Luria developed the ideas of his predecessors by controlled experimental observation on the role of language in children's adaptive behavior. As an illustration, it is well known that young infants find voluntary fine motor coordination quite difficult. For instance, a two-year-old child, when asked to press a rubber bulb, will press it continuously and will not be able to control the duration or frequency of pressing. Luria and his co-workers observed that children by the age of three could learn to press the bulb just twice if they accompanied the pressing by some vocalization, like "One, two," or some other externally corresponding sound pattern. This motor control broke down if the child was trained to verbalize his actions, saying to himself: "I will press twice." Consequently the phonetic rather than the semantic aspect of speech was important at age three as distinct from age four onward when semantic meaning can increasingly control motor behavior.

An additional observation showed that control of the start of a motor action by verbal cues was much earlier achieved than interruption of an ongoing activity by verbal instructions and that in the latter task reaction to the semantic aspect was crucial.

In Luria's investigation, the term "verbal control" takes on a clear but limited meaning, referring to the emission of overt or covert verbal responses which help in the execution of certain motor tasks. The following study suggests a much broader role for language in overall cognitive development.

Luria and Yudovich (1959) discovered twins who were severely retarded in speech development, owing to social isolation. They are described as follows.

> The twins' understanding of other people's speech was obviously unsatisfactory. They understood usual everyday speech when it directly referred to them but their comprehension of grammatically more complex speech which was not accompanied by explanatory actions was altogether imperfect. Speech which did not directly refer to them usually completely passed them by. . . . They never heard a book read, nor were they told stories, and they only listened to strangers talking if they heard their own names mentioned (Luria and Yudovich, 1959, p. 32).

They were separated from each other and given the opportunity to socialize and learn language in a normal way. One of the twins had special speech lessons. Dramatic improvement in speech and in the behavior patterns of both twins became evident after a relatively short time. The speech-trained child was claimed to perform better on a number of tests which seemed to be predominantly those on which he received special training. This study is now commonly cited as providing evidence for the necessity of speech in the development of thinking. Reference will be made to it again in Chapter XII where psychological observations are reported on another pair of twins, one of whom was hearing, the other deaf.

In general there can be little doubt that for Soviet scholars the second signal system as conceived by Pavlov is closely associated, if not actually identified, with the verbal language of society, and that intelligent behavior or thinking could well be explained in terms of silent, internalized speech.

Germany. Heinz Werner's thought is here treated as a separate school because Werner, although living in the United States for about 30 years until his death in 1964, during the days of strict behaviorism stayed somewhat on the periphery of American psychology and continued to develop the Austrian-German tradition. He is known for stressing the crucial importance of comparative-developmental aspects when studying human behavior. Like Vygotsky, he discovered a rich source of psychological knowledge in the systematic observation of the growing child.

Werner emphasized the organismic aspect of behavior and on this topic probably made his most original contribution to experimental psychology. He contended that any human behavior must be seen as rooted in a living organism, and issuing from the organism as an emergent whole reaction. Such a view was obviously incompatible with a stimulus-response model of human behavior. A meaningful transaction, whether in the perceiving of an object or in the utterance of words, is to be considered in its process of formation and is always related to ongoing sensory-motoric organismic activity.

In his last book in collaboration with Kaplan, Werner (1963) discusses symbolization and language behavior within this organismic-developmental framework. No attempt is made here to summarize such a volume, the fruit of many years' work, but some critical consideration can be given to the thoughts of these authors on the topic of the thinking-language relation.

First, signals are distinguished from symbols. Signals are elicitors of action, anticipating an event; however, the function of representing an event is unique to symbols. This distinction parallels an even more basic difference in mode of knowing. An animal is said to relate to an external state of affairs by reacting to it, while humans construct "cognitive objects." Signal behavior is thus related to an object-as-things-of-actions, while symbolization corresponds to objects-as-known. Animals are said to react to the signals of the environment, while man transforms his milieu into objects-to-be-known and orientates his action primarily toward the cognitive objects mediating between him and his physical milieu. Cognitive objects are directly related to symbolization since symbolizing enters into the construction of these "things-as-known."

The developmental beginnings of a known object are rooted in organismic sensory-motor reactions which Werner names schemas. Thus a child is said to have a schema of chair if he reacts differentially and functionally to a chair, even though he may not know the word. Some of the internal reactions may be measurable motoric-kinesthetic activities. The child acquires the meaning of the linguistic symbol "chair" when the underlying activity of schematization which regulates the schema of chair shapes the pattern of the sound sequence. The sound sequence constitutes the material aspect or the vehicle of the symbol. A symbol is thus on the one hand rooted in the organismic state corresponding to the known object and is at the same time indispensably interwoven with the construction of the cognitive object itself. One gets the distinct impression that for these authors the symbol is the means by which the schema is raised from a sensory-motor to a conceptual level of knowing.

Throughout the book the authors' concern is mainly with language. They emphasize that the acquisition and use of language cannot be an arbitrary learning of signals. They attribute to verbal language a unique quality as the symbol *par excellence* which becomes an inherent part of the mature concept. In the chapters where the authors are particularly concerned about the vehicle-referent relationship, one looks for some clarification of the relation of thinking and language. These expectations are not quite fulfilled since one is never sure whether "vehicle" relates to language and "referent" to thinking. But if vehicle means the symbol in its material aspect and referent the symbol in its meaning aspect, then the assumed reciprocal changes between vehicle and referent take place by definition of the terms: both denote the same event.

Other authors with important ideas, several of whom have

been mentioned, seem to theorize on the relation of thinking and language; but on closer inspection one finds that the explicit or implicit denotations of these two words are the same reality under two different aspects. If the terms language and thinking are a priori assumed to differ as little as the terms George Washington and the first president of the United States, one is bound to find a close relation, if not identity, between the terms. An empirically meaningful question of the relation between two concepts must first establish objectively distinct denotations for them.

This ends our partial view of the present state of the psychology of thinking and language, which for lack of a better name we have called "neobehavioral." No special section was devoted to Piaget's school which looms large on the present horizon. This omission will be repaired in Chapter XIII where we discuss a theory of cognitive development which does not place undue stress on language. Characteristically, Piaget is not considered part of psycholinguistics and for this reason also it is proper to deal with his school elsewhere.

If we now look back on the historical and contemporary context as represented by leading scholars in the field of thinking and language, we find with hardly a dissenting voice that *language* is considered the critical means enabling human intelligence to be what it is. Such a statement appears *prima facie* obvious and at the same time unassailable, because language is as universal as human nature and one cannot test the effect of an unchangeable condition. But we know now that language, as we know it, stops short of the deaf. Should we not be curious about the intellectual status of these language-deprived people?

Aside from concerning themselves with the deaf, psychologists should not be satisfied with the unclarified situation in the field of thinking. What is really meant by the word "language" as it is employed in its various forms, as second signal, symbol, verbal mediation, inner speech? Surely we place too great a burden upon one concept if we assume language to be the means, the end product, and possibly the content of thinking.

Linguists have long realized that the term language can refer to the abstract linguistic system of a language as described in books on grammar or syntax, and to the living language of people speaking or writing. While psychologists naturally use the term language in the second, behavioral aspect, they will eventually see the need for making many more distinctions within linguistic behavior.

Indeed, most writers who have employed the term language in connection with thinking have not unambiguously defined the term, and if hard pressed they may concede that by language they do not necessarily imply the verbal language of our society, but simply any kind of, possibly covert, system of symbols. Even if the term language is taken in the narrow sense of the natural language, how is the relation between language and thinking conceptualized? Do we think *with* words, *in* words or do we visualize or imaginatively hear words? Or does language merely provide training in, or better the opportunity for thinking? Again, is it the syntactical structure of language which is needed to make our thinking intelligent? Is it the social, historical aspect of the living language as a carrier of culture which affects the intellectual level of our thinking? Can there be an intelligent symbol without verbal support? What are the real denotations for the terms thinking, symbol, and language?

These and other questions of a similar kind force themselves upon one who probes deeply beneath the surface of existing writings. I admit these questions did not occur to me, as they have not occurred to most contemporary psychologists, until I was faced with an apparently thinking person who had no verbal language—the profoundly deaf person.

We shall therefore turn to the empirical investigation of

different aspects of deaf people's thinking behavior. If language is responsible for all that so many psychologists say it is, then we know what to expect about the level of performance from a linguistically deprived population! Be that as it may, a consideration of thinking in deaf people cannot but sharpen our distinctions, focus better our theoretical positions, and broaden the base from which our reasoning proceeds.

Science, for all its claim to the contrary, must start with some untested assumption of a philosophical nature. The psychological study of thinking has tended to assume the existence of a living language, itself a product of thinking. Perhaps we have been too engaged in writing a grammar of thinking, which like a linguistic grammar describes certain rather obvious aspects of language but which at the same time assumes on the part of the reader an intuitive understanding of the more basic questions concerning language. A serious consideration of deaf persons forces us to question and analyze these untested intuitive assumptions about the role of language in thinking. In so doing, insofar as the investigator must use nonverbal means of observing their thinking, the study of deaf persons may contribute in a unique way to our general knowledge of thinking and its relation to language.

Nonverbal Testing Methods

Observations in my work with the deaf have convinced me that, contrary to widespread opinion, intellectual functioning cannot depend basically upon language. Otherwise, how could the adult deaf come into possession of so many conceptual principles that deaf children struggle unsuccessfully to master through verbal training?

How could a theoretical position such as mine be tested empirically? From this question arose the research program, still in progress, the results of which are reported here.

At the outset it promised to be a challenging venture. Several rather large obstacles appeared immediately, some concerning the experimental study of intelligence in general and some, more specifically, concerned the particular problems involved in testing the deaf. The task, I realized, would be doubly difficult because, apart from the endeavors centered around IQ testing and measurements of test-based abilities, there is as yet no accepted theory of intelligence on which experimental investigations could be based. One would have to devise experimental tasks which would somehow appeal in turn to different characteristics of what is generally called "intelligent behavior."

As to the deaf themselves, one would be guilty of gross overgeneralization if one considered them as a homogeneous group. The same differences of ability, experience, and personality no doubt exist among them that are found in any other group. For this reason there is, strictly speaking, no such thing as a "psychology of the deaf" and we wished to avoid any such implication in our research.

There is one trait, however, most deaf persons do share. That is an objective and measurable lack of language skill. Thus it was appropriate to use deaf people as representing language-deficient subjects in experiments that investigated the role of language in thinking. In a particular process of selecting deaf subjects was used that restricted this assumption, this selection will be noted and the results of the experiments interpreted accordingly.

The first consideration in testing deaf persons is a very obvious one. Clearly, verbal tasks cannot be relied upon as accurate measurements of intelligence in language-deficient subjects. While not denying that within certain limits, when used and interpreted correctly, such tests may give some indication of a deaf person's performance level, we believe most standardized intelligence tests, relying heavily on verbal facility, would prove very inaccurate indices of cognitive ability. The question would immediately arise: Does the poorer performance of deaf subjects on such tasks indicate limited intelligence or merely the inability to understand the use of language?

Also, any standardized intelligence test depends for its validity on the assumption that a given subject is part of the sample on which the test was standardized. The deaf, of course, are not part of this sample.

In addition, we are now beginning to realize that verbal testing methods may give inaccurate results even with those not handicapped by hearing loss. One reason for this is the possibility of giving a right answer for a wrong reason. For example, a child may answer "fruit" to the question, "How are an apple and a pear alike?" The answer is correct, but may be merely the result of a linguistic habit linking the words "apple" and "pear" rather than a real knowledge of classes.

Another very important factor, now being increasingly recognized, is that verbal habits are subject to environmental circumstances. Children of so-called "culturally deprived" families are at a definite disadvantage here, but we cannot take their poorer performance as a clear indication of intellectual deficiency, for it may very well be the result of their very limited environment. Such children, far from knowing or seeking answers to questions, may not even have enough intellectual curiosity to realize there are questions to be asked.

As far as standardized nonverbal tasks are concerned, those few already in existence did not seem particularly well suited to our purposes. The majority of them measure perceptual or motor skills, while our main concern was with more advanced cognitive functioning. Though sometimes used in so-called performance tests of intelligence, such tests do not give very reliable results regarding thinking or reasoning ability. An example of such tests is Raven's Progressive Matrices, a promising tool but not yet sufficiently validated to determine what capacities are actually measured. In general, standardized tests of intelligence are by design limited to obtaining a certain score in relation to a normative sample and do not readily contribute to the basic questions underlying this study.

What was needed for our research were nonverbal methods for the scientific investigation of intelligent behavior. Would it be possible to devise nonverbal experimental situations which by common consent required intellectual functioning and which would therefore give some ground for the inference of intellectual ability?

By "nonverbal" I do not imply situations suspending all language behavior in the subject. Obviously this is impossible. In using this term, I mean tasks in which words are not used either as stimuli or as response, or as the criterion of success. Language in the sense of connected verbal language is not an essential part of the experimental situation. Linguistic competence is not assumed, and verbalization of any kind is discouraged.

I had to overcome the additional difficulty of ambiguity in nonverbal instructions, which at times made reliable interpretation of performances impossible. This was particularly important in reference to the deaf, for understanding of instructions is of course essential for correct response. When the deaf failed or did poorly in a given task, one has to consider the possibility that they did not understand what they were expected to do.

At first, I assumed that ability to discover a principle was an acceptable test of thinking ability. Some of the learning tasks to be reported here are discovery tasks. By "discovery" is meant the successful solution of a relatively unstructured problem through finding some relevant feature in a mass of irrelevant material. As nonverbal procedures do not permit explicit verbal instructions, the discovery aspect of a problem appeared to be a ready method of testing deaf people.

I soon saw, however, that discovery itself is often too undetermined, too elusive an event to serve as a reliable measurement of thinking. Sometimes it is the product of a chance happening rather than of intelligent operation, and a young child may perform better in this than the most sophisticated adult. Many aspects not related to intelligence may be involved in discovering an artificial principle, nor is mastery of the principle related to speed of discovery. For example, the principle of pointing to the second six-letter noun on a page does not imply a particularly difficult concept, yet it might take a long time for a person to discover it by trial and error, if he discovers it at all. *In fine,* the difficulty of discovering a concept may have no connection with the relative difficulty of the concept itself.

To overcome the above problems, I decided therefore to concentrate more on transfer-type tasks. These have an introductory task which is simple, to ensure that the subject understands what is expected. The subsequent second or transfer task, using familiar material in a new way, may then be taken as an index of cognitive performance. The person who on the first task has shown that he understands the instructions, is now called upon to apply the principle he has learned in a new situation. Thus one can observe how well the subject employs the principle despite new or interfering conditions making its use more difficult.

Transfer tasks also have the added advantage of minimizing or partially controlling other factors—motivational or personality characteristics—which may interfere with cognitive performance. Moreover, with such tasks one can at least partially control the subject's previous experience or lack of experience insofar as the first task affords some training and creates familiarity with the test situation.

In working out the series of tasks reported here we made use of material from various sources. Use was made of some learning tasks from the experimental laboratory (concept formation, reversal-learning, transposition) modified if necessary to suit the requirements. We also adapted some current verbal tests to nonverbal presentation, for example, the similarity type test of the Wechsler Scales. Throughout Piaget's work, a number of experiments are employed which purport to demonstrate the presence or absence of logical thinking. Although Piaget constantly used verbal instructions and verbal responses, it seemed that the essential requirement of the tasks was nonverbal and that the experiments could be modified so as to become nonverbal problem-solving tasks. Some of these are discussed in Chapter IX on Piaget-type tasks.

The experiments reported in this study were in five broad areas of thinking behavior: conceptual discovery and control; memory and perception; Piaget-type tests of conservation; logical classification; and verbal mediation. They are discussed in that order with the exception of verbal mediation which is discussed in Chapter XII. Chapter XI contains the conclusions concerning the previous experiments with the deaf. This separation from the previous experimental chapters is done primarily because mediation experiments largely proved negative, that is, no differences between deaf and hearing were observed. While no specific conclusions could be drawn about the deaf, the results are of theoretical import and together with the preceding summary of results on the deaf provide the impetus for the theoretical chapter (Chapter XIII) that follows.

CHAPTER VII

Concept Discovery and Control

*Experiment 1: Sameness, Symmetry,
and Opposition (Furth, 1961)*

If one observes that deaf pupils are being "taught" the meaning of the word 'opposite' in the intermediate grades (about the age of 14), and that they are having difficulty using the term correctly, one may wonder how such children would perform on a nonverbal task based on the principle of opposition.

The verbal concept of opposition should be quite familiar to hearing children beyond six years, as a study by Kreezer and Dallenbach (1929) showed. Our language employs many dimensions in terms of opposites: hot-cold, good-bad, long-short. Frequently the child learns the words denoting extremes before he learns words characterizing the dimension as such. In this way the child becomes acquainted naturally with the linguistic use of opposition and by age six can readily give correct verbal answers in connection with the word "opposite." Quite possibly, then, the frequent use of verbal opposites might give hearing children an advantage over deaf children even on a nonverbal task of opposites. But how would the deaf perform on other comparable tasks in which hearing children had no linguistic advantage?

At this point, N. Levy, who had collected data on non-verbal tasks of *Sameness* and *Symmetry,* suggested the use of these tasks with the deaf. For these two tasks, the correct principle or concept could be assumed to be as familiar or unfamiliar to the deaf as to the hearing children. The concept of "same," involved in the first task, is so primitive that workers with the deaf report there is no deaf child in school who does not have at least some gesture for this idea. On the basis of a study by Levy and Ridderheim, partially replicated here, it seemed reasonable to assume that hearing children before age 12 do not have the verbalized concept of "symmetry" readily available and should have, therefore, no linguistic advantage over deaf children on symmetry tasks.

Thus, there were three concept learning tasks, differing in relation to the language repertoire available in the subjects. For *Sameness,* deaf and hearing were alike insofar as they could both express this concept. For *Symmetry,* they were alike in not knowing the correct word, but for *Opposition,* they differed. The hearing knew and the deaf did not know its verbal use. It was thus expected that lack of language would not handicap deaf children in discovering the principles of sameness or symmetry, but might do so in attaining and using the principle of opposition.

SUBJECTS AND PROCEDURES

Pupils aged 7 to 12, from public and private schools for the deaf were used on this task, with 30 subjects in each of the six age groups. The hearing sample consisted of 180 children selected at random from five different grade schools and arranged in six groups of 30 each, also within the age groups from 7 to 12.

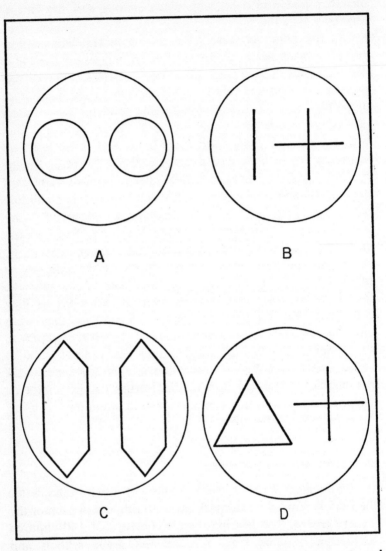

Figure 1. Sample of two pairs of stimuli for Sameness. A and C are correct choices.

The *Sameness* task consisted of a series of 40 different pairs of round tin covers with two simple figures drawn on each cover. The two figures on one of the covers were identical. On the other, the two were different. An illustration is given in Figure 1. Under the cover with identical figures, a checker was placed indicating to the child the correct choice. The criterion for success was 10 consecutive correct choices. The trials were terminated after the criterion was reached or with the first error after trial 30.

The *Symmetry* task consisted of 40 different pairs of 7 x 9 inch cards. Simple figures were drawn in heavy black ink on a white background. On one card of each pair, as shown in Figure 2, the figure to be rewarded was a symmetrical one, while on the other it was asymmetrical.

The *Opposition* task was in two parts: Acquisition and Transfer.

Opposition Acquisition. From a set of eight wooden discs ranging in diameter from ½ inch increasing in size in steps of ¼ inch to 2¼ inches, hidden from the child's view, four were selected in a fixed order and thrown at random on the table. The experimenter pointed either to the largest or the smallest disc. If he pointed to the largest, the child's task was to discover that he had to pick the smallest. If the smallest was chosen, the child was to pick the largest. A maximum of 36 trials was given, with the criterion of success six consecutive correct choices.

Opposition Transfer. To the children who succeeded on the first task, one uncorrected trial was given on each of six transfer dimensions: volume, length, number, brightness, position, and texture. The following materials were used:

1. *Volume.* Four wooden blocks ½ cu. in., ¾ cu., in., 1 cu. in., and 1¼ cu. in.

2. *Length.* Four wooden sticks ¾ in. square in width and 2 in., 3 in., 4 in., and 5 in. long.

79

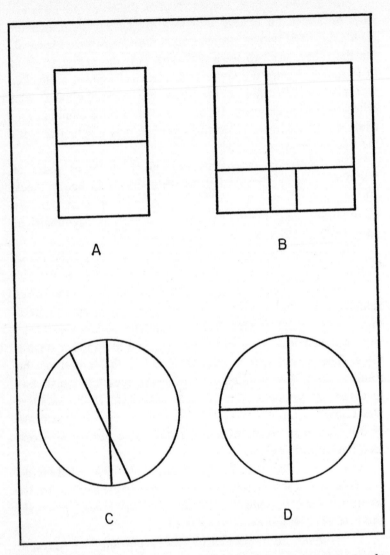

Figure 2. Sample of two pairs of stimuli for Symmetry. In the upper pair A is the correct choice, in the lower pair D is the correct choice.

3. *Number.* Five 1 sq. in. black domino-like blocks with 1, 2, 3, 4, and 5 white dots painted on them.

4. *Brightness.* Four white cards 3 in. x 5 in. with 1½ in. square painted on each one. The squares were shaded in four degrees of brightness, from light gray to black.

5. *Position.* (See Figure 3) Five white cards, 3 in. x 5 in., with a circle 1½ in. in diameter drawn on each one. The circle rested on a 1 in. line and a heavy dot was put in five different positions, one for each card: on the base line, to the left, on top, to the right, and in the center of the circle.

6. *Texture.* Four kinds of sandpaper, of four different qualities, Nos. 1, 2, 3, and 5 were pasted on a base, 3½ in. x 1½ in.

On all these transfer tasks, when the experimenter pointed to the stimulus on one extreme of the continuum of four or five stimuli, the child showed transfer for the concept by pointing to the opposite extreme.

RESULTS AND DISCUSSION

The results of this experiment, as summarized in Table 2, supported the original expectation. On the first two tasks, no consistent difference emerged, while on the *Opposition* task the deaf were poorer than the hearing at all age levels. Table 4, page 86, reveals more clearly the consistency of this difference at each age level and provides relevant data for the transfer test.

Here then, on a nonverbal concept attainment task, the same deaf children who had demonstrated equality on the *Sameness* and *Symmetry* tasks were consistently below the hearing children on *Opposition* tasks.

The inferiority of the deaf children on one specific concept could be attributed to the assumption that verbal language, by constantly referring to opposites, gives hearing children a specific advantage, even on a nonverbal task of

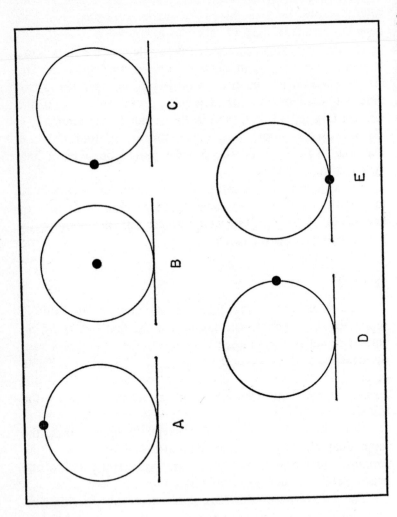

Transfer. The examiner points to A, the child should point

opposites. At this point one may wonder how general such a phenomenon is, i.e., whether there are many other specific concepts on which the deaf would emerge as inferior? This remains to be discovered through further research rather than by speculation. Moreover, this study says nothing about the duration of this deficiency, whether adult deaf also suffer from it or not. Mainly, however, this study demonstrated that linguistic experience or habits may aid in the discovery of a specific concept without notably influencing other concepts.

Concerning the easy success on opposites on the part of the hearing, this seems to be an appropriate example of what Vygotsky (1962) called pseudo-concepts, which are created through linguistic usage. Verbal behavior of young children may at times give the impression of mastery of a certain concept, but a closer look reveals that the child has primarily learned to use a verbal term correctly in linguistic associations. A child may, for instance, use the word "sufficient" correctly, but his inability to distinguish "full" from "sufficient" would demonstrate his ignorance of the mature concept. Likewise, it is improbable that the seven-year-old children in the experiment had actually mastered the concept of opposite. We may simply suppose that the hearing were aided in performing the task by thorough familiarity with language, without making any inference about the conceptual maturity of their development.

Table 2—Number of Successful Hearing and Deaf Subjects on Concept Learning Tasks in Each Age Group (30 subjects in each age group)

Age	SAMENESS		SYMMETRY		OPPOSITION	
	Hearing	Deaf	Hearing	Deaf	Hearing	Deaf
7	4	7	6	4	29	14
8	6	16	4	11	26	19
9	12	16	8	19	28	23
10	11	20	12	21	30	28
11	13	11	14	11	30	28
12	22	15	21	19	30	27
Total	68	85	65	85	173	139

Experiment 2: A Replication of the Sameness, Symmetry and Opposition Task with Retarded Children (*Milgram and Furth, 1963*)

In this experiment, educable retarded children were the subjects. We considered that just as the deaf child is limited in language experience, the retarded child is limited also in his ability to use whatever language experience he may have for the conceptual grasp of situations. Before comparing the performance of the retarded group on the three concept tasks, we predicted that on *Sameness* and *Symmetry* tasks the retarded children would perform as well as normal children of comparable mental age. We expected, however, that the retarded would perform less well on the *Opposition* acquisition and *Opposition* transfer tasks than normal children of comparable MA (mental age).

SUBJECTS AND PROCEDURE

The tasks were the same as those described in the preceding experiment. Those tested were children, age 9 to 17, who either attended special classes in a large metropolitan school system or a small private institution for the educable retarded. The IQ range on Stanford-Binet Form L, given within one year of our study, was 50–75. No children with serious visual, aural, or motor defects were included. All could speak with fair fluency, lived at home and attended full time classes, and were considered educable by school authorities.

The normal controls were groups of 30 each of children, age 7, 8, and 10, chosen from the hearing subjects of the preceding experiment. In addition, there were 16 normal children age 6. All were from low middle-class neighborhoods and presumably of average or slightly above average ability. The retarded children were divided into four groups of 16 each, with average MA's of 5.8, 7, 8.3, and 9.9 respectively, which

84

were compared with groups of normal children of corresponding chronological age. There were equal numbers of boys and girls.

RESULTS AND DISCUSSION

The performance of educable retarded children on this task paralleled in a striking fashion that of the deaf in the previous experiment. While the retarded subjects were not inferior to normal children of comparable MA on concept tasks in which language experience was not considered relevant, they were less adept both in attaining the language-relevant concept and in applying it to transfer tasks. Actually the retarded group did better than the control group on the *Symmetry* task, just as in the previous experiment the deaf were superior to the hearing on this particular problem.

The prediction that educable retarded children compared with normal children of similar MA would perform in essentially the same manner was borne out by the results.

It should be stressed that retarded and normal children were equated not on chronological age but on mental age. Thus subjects in the retarded group with a mental age of six were actually about nine years old. The fact that the retarded performed on a comparative level on *Sameness* and *Symmetry* merely confirmed that the nine year olds had a mental age of six. It may be of interest to note that children with retardation associated with brain damage or constitutional abnormality performed on a level comparable to the cultural-familial retarded group.

As Tables 3 and 4 show, the retarded perform even lower than their average low level when the task involves attainment and application of a concept for which linguistic usage provides some added advantage. In other words, the retarded may comprehend the meaning of a word as shown by a simple vocabulary test, but they are less skilled than

85

normal children in using the linguistic medium for the solution of conceptual tasks. The following study (Experiment 3: Discovery of Similarities) intended to show this point more clearly.

Table 3—Percentage of Subjects Reaching Criterion on Concept Learning Tasks

MA	SAMENESS		SYMMETRY		OPPOSITION	
	Normal	Retarded	Normal	Retarded	Normal	Retarded
6	37.5	18.7	12.5	12.5	68.7	37.5
7	13.3	31.2	20.0	43.7	96.9	81.2
8	20.0	37.5	13.3	43.7	86.7	62.5
10	36.7	31.2	40.0	56.2	100.0	56.2
Total	25.5	29.7	22.6	39.1	90.6	59.4

Table 4—Mean Transferred Responses of Control, Retarded and Deaf Subjects on Opposition Transfer

MA	CONTROL		RETARDED		DEAF	
	N*	Response	N*	Response	N*	Response
6	11	3.7	6	3.2	—	—
7	29	4.0	13	3.6	14	3.2
8	26	4.5	10	3.9	19	3.2
10	30	5.2	9	4.8	28	4.4
Total	96	4.5	38	3.9	61	3.8

* Number of subjects who were successful on the prior task of Opposition Acquisition from a total N = 30 for each age level of Controls and Deaf, (except N = 16 for Controls, age 6); and from a total N = 16 for each age level of Retarded.

Experiment 3: Discovery of Similarities
(Furth and Milgram, 1965)

Similarity-type tests are among those most commonly used in evaluating so-called "abstract" intelligence. For example, a child may be asked: "How are a pencil and a typewriter alike?" His correct response is assumed to indicate his conceptual grasp of what these objects have in common. We devised a nonverbal modification of such a test to determine the performance of subjects with differing degrees of linguistic ability. It is noteworthy that previously low scores on such verbal similarity tasks have been considered evidence that the deaf are poor in "abstract" thinking.

At the same time, the general purpose of this investigation was to isolate conceptual or class knowledge from antecedent or subsequent verbal factors, and to assess the role and interaction of such linguistic variables in the solution of this conceptual task. The study attempted to control for three main variables:

1. The input or receptive stage, by using words vs. pictures as stimuli;
2. The output or expressive stage, by requiring a verbal statement vs. merely pointing;
3. Linguistic experience, by employing three groups in descending order of verbal ability:
   (a) Hearing children of normal intelligence,
   (b) Hearing children educably retarded,
   (c) Deaf children of normal intelligence.

PROCEDURE

1. *Picture Sorting (PS)*. The nonverbal similarity test took the form of picture sorting. The materials used were a series of 18 sets of seven pictures each, drawn with black pencil on 3 x 5 white cards and easily recognizable as pictures of common objects or situations. For instance, three pictures of a series illustrated a common name (shoes, fruit, building); a common function (cleaning, measuring, writing); a common material (glass, metal, etc.); a common situation (motion, natural scenery) or common shape (spherical).

Discovery of the correct concept on the first seven sets (*Part 1*) was perceptually easy to facilitate understanding of the nature of the task by deaf children. The 11 remaining sets (*Part 2*) were generally more difficult to solve because of more difficult concepts as well as the perceptual pull of misleading part solutions, for example:

87

Pear, Table, Chair, *Apple,* Pail, *Cherry,* Cat.

Bathroom scale, Pencil, *Stopwatch,* Refrigerator, Bottle of glue, *Ruler,* Skyscraper.

The seven pictures of a set were placed in predetermined order on the table, four cards in the top row and the next three below. The child was instructed by word and gesture to pick out the "three cards that go together." Further verbalization was kept to a minimum. Generally the deaf subjects caught on to the gestured instruction quite readily. Throughout the sorting task the experimenter corrected wrong choices by pointing to the appropriate pictures. Only PS was given to the deaf, this being the sole task with no verbal component, while the following three tests were given also to all the hearing children.

2. *Word Sorting (WS).* As we were interested in learning how the PS test would relate to verbal similarity tests, we also devised a verbal form of the PS task which is here called WS. WS and PS tasks were similar on the response side but differed on the input side. Instead of a set of seven pictures, the child saw seven cards before him with words written on them. The experimenter read the words distinctly to the child. The response, just as in the PS task, was a nonverbal one, the child pointing to three cards. In order to evaluate correctly the influence of verbal response, we added verbalization to both these tasks. This is indicated respectively by PV (Picture Verbalization) and WV (Word Verbalization).

The verbalization tasks were presented to all hearing subjects after they had finished the respective sorting task. Those subjects who were first given PS continued with PV, while those who had done WS first were then given WV.

3. *Picture Verbalization (PV).* The children were shown the 18 sets of three pictures illustrating a concept, one set at a time. They were asked:

"Tell me how these go together," or "In which way are these the same?"

88

4. *Word Verbalization* (*WV*). For this task the experimenter placed the three appropriate cards before the child and read the words which were written on them aloud, as part of the question: "Tell me in which way are Boot, Shoe, and Slipper alike?" All responses were recorded and no corrections were given.

Two separate experiments were actually performed. Experiment 1 compared deaf and hearing subjects at age levels eight and sixteen on PS, while Experiment 2 presented all four conditions of the classification task (PS, PV, WS, WV) to two groups of normal and retarded children with MA 9.

RESULTS AND DISCUSSION

Table 5 indicates the mean score of all groups in Experiments 1 and 2. These scores are based on 18 possible choices. Hence there is a maximum score of 18. In Experiment 1 the younger deaf subjects generally were poorer than hearing children of the same age, while the older deaf proved equal to their hearing peers. A further analysis of the total score showed that for the introductory *Part 1,* the deaf made 4.68 correct responses as compared with 6.21 for the hearing. For

Table 5—Mean Correct Choices on Classification Tasks

			EXPERIMENT 1	
Subjects	N	Age	Picture Sorting	
Deaf	25	8	8.88	
Control	24	8	12.08	
Deaf	12	16	14.75	
Control	12	16	14.84	
			EXPERIMENT 2	
Subjects	N	Age	Picture Sorting	Picture Verbalization
Retarded	19	MA 9	12.79	12.05
Control	19	CA 9	12.47	9.97
Subjects	N	Age	Word Sorting	Word Verbalization
Retarded	19	MA 9	5.21	7.44
Control	19	CA 9	7.79	9.26

Part 2, the respective scores were 4.20 and 5.87. Both comparisons were significant.

The results of the second experiment can be briefly summarized by referring to Table 5. PS was easiest for both the normal and retarded children, and the addition of verbal factors generally led to poorer performance. Verbal requirements on the input side were relatively harder than on the output side. This is shown by the lowest score, which was on WS, a task which required verbal comprehension and utilization of 7 words at one time but no verbal response. With words as input, sorting of 7 words in WS was harder than verbalization to 3 words in WV. In contrast, with pictures as input, PS and PV were equally difficult for normal children, but not for the retarded. The latter found sorting of 7 pictures in PS easier than verbalization to 3 pictures in PV, so that for the retarded there emerged a clear interaction. With words, the verbalization task was easier than the sorting task, while with pictures, the sorting task was easier than the verbalization task. Looking at the two subject groups, we observe that the retarded performed as well as the MA controls on the nonverbal task of PS, but were inferior on all three other conditions in proportion to the increased linguistic difficulty.

If we consider first the results of the second experiment, granting that as a conceptual task PS is nonverbal, then we have here a situation in which the verbal factors are experimentally isolated from what we may call pure conceptual factors. The substitution of verbal instead of pictorial elements on the input side (PS vs. WS, PV vs. WV) made a similar conceptual task more difficult for both groups, especially for the retarded. In particular, the poor performance of the retarded on all tasks except PS could lead an uncritical observer to the conclusion that the retarded are deficient in conceptual knowledge. Given the comparative data with normal and control data on PS, it seems more reasonable to attribute the lowered performance of the retarded to a specific difficulty in handling the linguistic medium. The fact that the retarded apparently possess adequate conceptual knowledge is demonstrated by their equivalent performance on PS. Thus we may conclude that PS is a relatively pure measure of concept knowledge, not dependent upon linguistic proficiency. This is particularly true in comparison with the other conditions which include verbal elements and in large part test linguistic and not merely conceptual skill.

In the light of this discussion, the outcome of Experiment 1 with the deaf becomes more understandable. The retardation of the eight-year-old deaf group cannot be related simply to a lack of comprehension of instructions. In that case, only the performance on the initial *Part 1* should be lowered and by trial 8 any hesitancy due to lack of comprehension should have vanished. As was pointed out, however, the younger deaf were also poorer on *Part 2*.

At the 16 year level, no difference in performance was noted. Whatever retardation existed at the 8 year level in the deaf child is no longer evident by the time he reaches 16. This improvement cannot be generalized at this point with any degree of confidence because of the possibility that the task may generally have been too easy for the older group.

Nevertheless, one is prompted to ask: Is this retardation at the 8-year-old level due to linguistic deficiency? If this same task had not been given to the retarded, or given only in verbal fashion, it would have been easy to conclude that the deaf perform less well because of their linguistic deficiency even on a nonverbal conceptual task. Here is a case illustrating the fact that careful control is needed in experiments with the deaf before conclusions are drawn. In cases where their performance is inferior, great care must be taken to distinguish exactly what factor may be responsible. The results obtained in Experiment 2 with the retarded should help to clarify the situation.

91

In the *Opposition* study, it has already been demonstrated that the retarded child performs very poorly on tasks in which the verbal component is of possible importance to success. How then do these same retarded children perform on *Similarities?* When one compares nine-year-old normal children with retarded children of MA 9, the results are clear. On PS the retarded were equal to the normal. On all other tasks where a verbal factor was part of the procedure, they were poorer, and they were particularly poor on WS where verbal input was of paramount importance.

These results seem to indicate that verbal factors were not important on the PS task. Consequently one is justified in suggesting that it was not strictly lack of language that caused the deaf to do less well on PS. Perhaps the result is related to their restricted experience that makes them less adroit in tasks of discovery.

On this task at least the handicap is not permanent. Somewhere in the process of growing up, these deaf children "catch up" so that in adult life, or even in adolescence, they can do as well in this area as others not thus handicapped.

Evidently, the term "restricted experience" needs a firmer empirical anchorage, not so much in regard to its objective existence, observable in nearly every family with a deaf child, but in its causal connection with cognitive deficit. Further studies are reported later on in this work to cast some light on the "restricted experience" concept.

Experiment 4: Conceptual Discovery and Control (*Furth, 1963b*)

A pictorial choice task enabled us to observe classificatory behavior under the control of one concept. In this experiment, the main requirement was the consistent selection of two pictures illustrating the Part-Whole concept in spite of the presence of other reasonable choices.

Our purpose in designing this task was to learn more about the relation between nonverbal conceptual behavior under the aspect of conceptual control and the variables of age, intelligence, and verbal language. The ages of the subjects ranged from 6 to 14 years and within each age group the performance of children of varying intelligence was studied. Thus we were able to evaluate IQ and MA in relation to this nonverbal task. We attempted further to measure the influence of language by comparing deaf with hearing children at each age level and by asking hearing children to verbalize the principle by which they solved the problem.

SUBJECTS AND PROCEDURE

The hearing children who participated in this experiment came from Grades one to five and Grade ten of several parochial schools. Divided into six groups on the basis of age—6 years, 7 years, 8 years, 10 years, and 14 years—there were in each of the groups 36, 51, 59, 62, and 100 subjects respectively. The deaf subjects were chosen according to availability from various schools for the deaf, and in each age group corresponding to the above there were 16, 11, 14, 20, 13, and 41 children.

An artist drew twenty sets of five pictures each with black pencil on 3 x 5 inch white cards. In each set only two drawings illustrated the Part-Whole relation and these two were the "correct" choices. Several other reasonable combinations according to class, function, or experiential association were included in each set. These related pictures, providing a strong pull of misleading perceptual associations, would, we believed, effectively establish whether or not the subjects had firmly grasped the specific principle of Part-Whole. In one set, there were, for example, Eyeglasses, Face, Book, Hat, and Ear.

93

While the pictures of Face and Ear were the only correct choice according to the Part-Whole principle, other reasonable choices which might interfere with the correct selection were: Eye-glasses and Book, Hat and Face, etc. The first 13 sets were used as learning trials while sets 14 to 20 served as uncorrected criterion trials.

The experimenter placed five pictures of one set on the table in random order and without further explanation indicated to the child that he should pick up or point out two of the five. After the last trial, the hearing child was asked to explain, if he could, the principle of his choices.

RESULTS AND DISCUSSION

The observations are summarized in Table 6, below, which present the mean error of hearing subjects of above and below average IQ as well as the scores of the total hearing and deaf sample according to chronological age. A statistical analysis of these data revealed the following three main results:

There was an overall trend for performances to improve with age, but this relation was not pronounced and not consistent from year to year. On the other hand, IQ was a very significant factor, with high IQ subjects consistently making less errors than low IQ subjects at each age level. Moreover, the performance of the deaf subjects closely approximated the performance of the hearing subjects.

Table 6—Mean Error of Groups on Criterion Trials as a Function of Age and IQ

Group		6	7	8	9	10	14
Hearing	High IQ*	—	3.5	2.2	2.7	1.4	1.9
	Low IQ*	—	5.3	4.5	4.0	3.2	3.0
	Total	3.9	4.1	3.4	3.4	2.4	2.2
Deaf		4.1	4.0	3.6	3.0	2.9	2.1

* Based on 10 Ss each randomly selected from the five age groups; the high group's IQ ranged between 105 and 115; the low group's IQ between 85 and 95.

Concerning post-test verbalization, it was found that the younger hearing groups were quite unable to explain their selections, even most of the fifth-graders replying merely: "I can't tell." Of 115 subjects 14 and 15 years old tested, 22 gave this answer, while 46 said something vague such as "go together—belong"; 30 mentioned "needed" or "repeated," while only 17 used the correct verbal term "part." Table 7, below, shows the number of errors subjects in these categories made on the seven criterion trials. It can be observed that the correspondence between correct verbalization and consistency of performance is by no means perfect or even close.

Table 7—Number of Subjects Making a Specified Number of Errors on Seven Criterion Trials as Related to Type of Verbalization

Verbalization	NUMBER OF ERRORS					
	0	*1*	*2*	*3*	*4*	*5*
Part	5	5	5	2	0	0
Needed	7	4	6	3	4	6
Go together	5	3	10	16	9	3
Can't tell	2	6	6	5	1	2

The major requirement of this task, in addition to discovering the principle of choice, namely the Part-Whole relation, was for the child to adhere to the concept in spite of competing pulls in other directions. It was found that even the younger children had little difficulty in discovering the principle and made relatively few errors during the learning trials. This substantiated the results reported on a verbal task by Schooley and Hartman in 1937. However, subjects made more errors in the later criterion trials, when they chose two pictures strongly associated by some principle other than Part-Whole. Their lack of conceptual control was shown by their inability to adhere consistently to the one relevant concept.

Results further showed that hearing children of high IQ performed consistently better than those of low IQ, the age factor apparently being of less importance than the IQ. This is illustrated in Table 6 by the fact that the mean score of 2.2 of the high IQ group at age 8 is comparable to the performance level of the average 14 year old group (2.1).

The nature of this task may perhaps be best described in relation to what Luria (1961) has called "verbal control." Luria, using verbal instructions, based his conclusions on observation of motoric behavior as a function of concomitant verbal behavior. It is here suggested that the term "conceptual control" would be appropriate for this experiment and in general more inclusive than Luria's "verbal control."

The term "conceptual control" seems to have the additional advantage of expressing—as unequivocally as one's definition of the word "conceptual" permits—a basic condition from which intelligent behavior is inferred. Reference is here made to the aspect of an internal mediation which is postulated between the external stimuli and the response. Thinking becomes manifest to the behavioral observer when behavior is apparently not under the adequate control of an external stimulus but internally controlled. Such inner control is especially obvious when, as in this study, there are external interfering pulls which by themselves would direct behavior away from its internal conceptual rule. In that case, one could justifiably use the term "abstract attitude" to point out that the concrete situational aspect had less control over behavior than inner activity which can be termed "conceptual."

Although the Part-Whole concept cannot be considered an abstraction of a high order, the ability to control behavior thereby would appear to be a form of abstract behavior. The results of this study imply that this abstract, conceptually controlled behavior, is largely independent of verbal behavior, whether we think of language in terms of general verbal experience or as specifically facilitating and controlling a given task. Deaf children, known to be minimally exposed to verbal experience, performed very much as did their hearing peers. The hearing children, on the other hand, found it impossible or very difficult to verbalize their rule of behavior and even when they did so, the relation of verbalization to performance was at best tenuous. Many of them even verbalized wrongly, while performing correctly for the most part. By contrast, of the 17 who did verbalize correctly, only five were able to consistently make the right choice on the criterion trials.

CHAPTER VIII

Memory and Perception

Memory and perception have at times been linked to verbal capacity. It has been suggested that covert verbalization of items-to-be-recognized substantially contributes to better performance. In particular, some previous investigators found deaf persons deficient on these tests as compared to hearing controls, and believed that these findings confirmed the link between verbal language and mnemonic or perceptual ability. Since past results were by no means consistent, we examined the immediate memory of the deaf in one investigation, and some basic attributes of visual perception in another.

Experiment 5: Visual Memory Span
(Olsson and Furth)

The purpose of this study was to compare deaf and hearing persons at two age levels on various memory span tasks which differed in verbal association value. Span tasks, familiar through their use in many intelligence test scales, measure the ability of a person to retain a certain number of discrete items for immediate recall. The most popular span test is auditory digit span which requires the subject to repeat the heard sequence of digits, e.g., 7– 4– 2– 8– 3– 5. It is called immediate memory, because the performance is an immediate repetition of the presented stimuli without explicit training or rehearsal. Association value refers to the ease with which certain stimuli arouse verbal associations.

Digit span tasks, even if presented visually, are of course highly verbal, and any person seeing the symbol "3" will rapidly associate the word "three." On the other hand, visual nonsense figures do not so easily elicit associations. Two kinds of nonsense figures were employed, those in which verbal associations were relatively easy (high association value) and those with relatively difficult verbal associations (low association value). Moreover, the stimuli for these memory tasks were presented in two different ways, simultaneously and successively.

Thus there were three span tasks, one for visually presented digits and two for nonsense figures with a set of high and a set of low association value. All three tasks were given in simultaneous and successive presentation to adult and adolescent hearing and deaf persons. It was thought that the possible influence of verbal activity would become manifest in a digit span task, which is highly verbal. Moreover, insofar as the deaf are less verbal, one would expect them to be less influenced than the hearing by the different association values on the memory task with forms.

Subjects and Procedure

The subjects for the adolescent groups were 30 deaf students within an age range of 12 to 16, half from a residential and half from a day school for the deaf. They were selected

99

in this manner to improve the representativeness of sampling rather than with a view toward any expected differences in memory performance. Fifteen hearing pupils of comparable age formed the control group.

For the adult groups, 16 deaf persons from a club for the deaf were compared to 16 hearing persons. All hearing and deaf groups were matched on IQ and both sexes were approximately evenly distributed.

The Memory Span for Digits task (MSD) was borrowed from the WAIS and the Wechsler Memory Scale, the former being used for successive presentation of digits, and the latter for simultaneous presentation. Each type of presentation consisted of two sets of 3 through 9 digits.

The Memory Span for Forms task (MSF) consisted of 50 forms grouped into high and low association sets. Each set contained series of 3, 4, 5, 6, and 7 forms. A total of ten series was used, five series from 3 to 7 forms apiece in the high and low association sets.

The association value of the forms had been previously determined by having them rated by a group of 45 college students. The 25 forms highest in association value were placed in the high association set, and the 25 forms lowest in association value in the low association set. The series of forms within each set were approximately equated in average association value.

Testing was done in small groups of 8 to 11 subjects and all groups followed a similar procedure. Slides of digits and forms were projected on a screen by means of an automatic slide projector.

In the MSD task, the digits were presented successively with 1 sec. exposure time and 2.2 sec. between each exposure. The subjects were told to write the digits in the exact order of presentation as soon as the series ended, but because of the difficulty in communicating with the deaf, no hard and fast standardization of instructions was attempted. Both written and spoken directions, as well as demonstrations, were used. The first series of three digits was used as an example and the answers to this were checked to make certain the subjects understood what was expected of them. During the entire procedure the examiner observed whether the subjects understood and were attending to the task.

The digits were then presented simultaneously, again with instructions and a demonstration using the first three digit series. Exposure time for each series was 1 sec. for each digit in the series, i.e., exposure time in seconds equaled the number of digits in the series.

With the MSF task, each group of subjects had been divided into two sub-groups, one of which received the successive presentation before the simultaneous, and the other received them in reverse order. Within each type of presentation, the high and low association series alternated (e.g., first the high association 3 form series, then the low association 3 form series, then the high association 4 form series, etc.). Instructions given were similar to those for the MSD task.

Each subject received a packet of 20 envelopes containing facsimiles of the forms for each series. They were told, as well as shown by demonstration, that forms would be projected on the screen in a particular order and that after the presentation, they were to take the facsimiles of the forms shown on the screen from the proper envelope and put them in the order of presentation from left to right on the table.

For the first two series (high and low association of 3 forms), the examiner checked the order of the forms for all subjects and made certain they understood the task. After the subjects had put the forms in order, they were shown how to pick them up in order by starting at the left, proceeding to the right, and placing each preceding form on top of the next. They were then to put the forms back into their respective envelopes.

101

In the successive presentation, the exposure time for each form was 2 sec. with 2.2 sec. between each exposure. The exposure times for the simultaneous presentation of the various series were 8, 10, 12, 14, and 16 sec. for the 3, 4, 5, 6, and 7 form series respectively.

RESULTS AND DISCUSSION

In both Memory Span tasks, the subject's score was the highest series of elements (either digits or forms) remembered in exact order of presentation.

Table 8 shows mean span scores for hearing and deaf groups on both types of memory task.

Table 8—Mean Visual Span Score

Subjects	DIGITS		HIGH ASSOCIATION FORMS		LOW ASSOCIATION FORMS	
	Simultaneous	Successive	Simultaneous	Successive	Simultaneous	Successive
Adolescents						
Hearing	8.27	7.80	5.87	5.67	4.07	4.47
Deaf	6.47	6.13	5.93	5.47	4.76	4.06
Adults						
Hearing	8.25	7.19	5.13	4.94	3.94	3.75
Deaf	6.38	5.56	5.44	4.69	4.19	3.75

These results may be summarized under four points:
1. The deaf differed minimally from the hearing on MSF, while on MSD they were consistently poorer.
2. High association helped the deaf as much as it helped the hearing.
3. Simultaneous presentation was in general easier than successive, and for MSF there was some slight indication that the deaf did somewhat better than the hearing on the simultaneous presentation, while the hearing did better than the deaf on successive presentation.
4. Adolescents did better than adults.

It should be added that residential and day school deaf groups performed alike on MSF, while on MSD, due to a technical error, only the scores of day school deaf could be utilized.

The first point presents an interesting contrast between memory for digits and for forms. On the latter task, deaf and hearing persons generally performed alike. This held true for children and for adults, as well as for both simultaneous and successive presentation of nonsense forms. On visual digits, however, the deaf did not remember as well as the hearing at either of the two age levels tested. Insofar as digits were assumed to be the most verbal of the span tasks, one may at first sight interpret these results as strengthening the notion that verbal ability helps memory when words are available.

Regarding the second point, in line with this reasoning one might have expected that high association would be of greater help to the hearing than to the deaf, since association value was based on verbal relationships. Insofar, however, as the high association and low association series had similar effects on both deaf and hearing subjects, verbal associations apparently did not contribute much to better memory performance in the area of visual forms. It may be rather that high association forms are more related to the familiar, and for that reason are both easier to remember and have more readily available verbal association. In any case, familiarity was of equal help to the deaf and hearing. Could familiarity or past experience be reasonably invoked with regard to the deficient performance of deaf subjects on digits?

Coming to the third point, it should be noted that digits as such are familiar to deaf people. They recognize digits and know manual signs for them, using the fingers to indicate any number. Consequently, it does not seem reasonable to assume that articulation as such helped the hearing because the deaf too could readily use their fingers to indicate a particular digit. However, consider the continuous practice with digits to

103

which the hearing are exposed. Academic subjects like mathematics and history, as well as every day activities such as using the telephone, provide for the hearing child constant and extensive practice in remembering digits, while the deaf child because of his linguistic handicap has minimal opportunity to practice memory for numbers.

The influence of constant training is dramatically exemplified in the case of blind adolescents. In testing them I observed that they had a digit span far above the average of their seeing peers, yet no one would suggest that blindness in itself increases memory ability. Obviously, because of the difficulty or impossibility of writing down or looking up numbers, the sightless person must remember them and consequently has much more practice in this than the seeing person who can readily refer to written information. Likewise, the fact that the deaf subjects did not perform as well on the digit span task should not lead to the immediate conclusion that the deaf have a poorer memory because of language deficiency.

Concerning the fourth point, an interesting development was the superiority of the adolescent over adult groups on all parts of this experiment, including both the deaf and the hearing. This result agrees with average scores on standardized tests.

It is, moreover, remarkable that the deaf and hearing subjects were alike, not only in age trends, but also in mode of presentation. It could have been expected that successive presentation was more dependent on verbalization than simultaneous presentation, and therefore greater differences could have emerged between hearing and deaf persons with regard to mode of presentation than are indicated in the third point of the results. Such overall similarity in memory performance argues for basically similar internal strategies for immediate memory—whatever they are—in persons who know and those who do not know a verbal language.

Experiment 6: Gestalt Laws in Visual Perception
(Furth and Mendez, 1963)

The role of language in the reproduction of visual stimuli was another area to be studied against the background of previous research in this field. On one hand, there are psychologists who, without denying the influence of language, believe that the organization of percepts is an autonomous activity perfected through the process of maturation.

Others have stressed the role of language. For example, some have maintained that changes in the reproduction of visual forms are determined by internal cues from a verbal analysis during perception. Other researchers studied the role of external verbal stimulation in the reconstruction of forms. The experiment described here was intended to provide further evidence about the perceptual activities of deaf persons with respect to some quite fundamental modes of visual perception. These have been termed *Gestalt* laws after the German school of psychology that emphasized the tendency of the human mind to perceive objects in terms of structural wholes and not as a collection of disparate elements. The use of both deaf and hearing subjects within two age groups allowed us to compare subjects at different levels of maturation and verbal experience.

SUBJECTS AND PROCEDURE

An attempt was made to equate the subjects not only in terms of age (two groups with a mean age of 16 years and 9 years), but also with regard to intelligence. However, due to the various means used in measuring this factor, the equating of the groups was at best quite crude. The subjects constituted a normally distributed sample with a mean IQ of 100 for each of the four groups. Each group was about equally divided as to sex. The deaf subjects were also subdivided according to reading ability.

In this task the figures were patterned after those generally employed to illustrate *Gestalt* principles of perceptual organization (See samples in Figure 4). The purpose in using these figures was to present them to the subjects with a minimum of verbal instruction. These figures were presented, in an order accentuating the *Gestalt* principle involved, on a memory-drum for 1 sec. each. Time was allowed for immediate reproduction on a fresh sheet of paper after each exposure.

Proximity. To investigate this principle, a series of drawings was used in which six parallel lines gradually separated into pairs. In the first drawing shown, the lines were equidistant. In those following, the space between the neighboring pairs was increased by 1/64 in. until the difference reached a ratio of 2 to 1.

Closure. The closure principle was observed in the organization of a percept as a letter of the alphabet and a complete geometrical figure.

1. Letter. A mutilated letter "E" was shown which required five steps for completion. After step 2, it was pointed out to all subjects that they were to see a letter of the alphabet. Thus the subjects were scored for recognition of the letter rather than for closure of gaps in the reproduction.

2. Geometrical Figure. A parallelogram with a bisecting line was presented in three steps. In step 1, the bisecting line stopped 1/16 in. short of the angles of the figure at either end, and one of the angles was open by 1/8 in.

Good Form. A letter of the alphabet and a geometrical figure were used.

1. Letter. A letter "C" was presented in two series, one ascending (steps 1, 2, 3), and one descending (steps 3, 2, 1). On the ascending series a protrusion in the center of the letter gradually disappeared. On the descending series, the lower

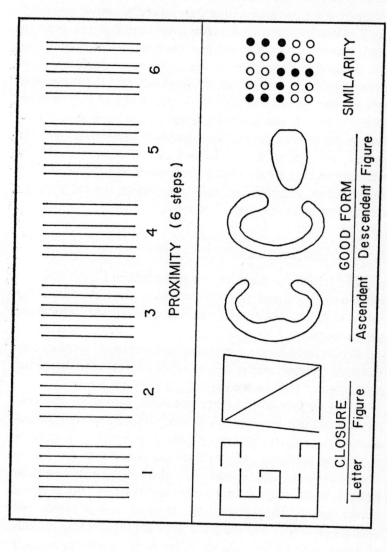

Figure 4. Gestalt drawings. All steps are shown for Proximity. The other six tasks are illustrated by selected samples. Letter Closure shows step 4, Similarity shows step 5, the remaining tasks are represented by step 1 in their respective series.

107

branch of the letter was gradually shortened. In contrast to all other tasks, the descending series can more properly be considered a discrimination rather than a *Gestalt* task.

2. Geometrical Figure. An oval-shaped figure with a blunt gradually rounding-out end was presented in three steps.

Similarity. To investigate the principle of similarity, in a square figure, composed of 25 small circles, a pattern was made to emerge progressively by deeper shades of gray in some of the circles. A training sample was shown immediately preceding the task as part of the nonverbal instructions. In this sample, the shaded circles formed an "X" and the subjects were shown that all they had to reproduce was the letter "X." In the actual experimental task, the pattern formed a figure closely resembling the Greek letter Psi.

RESULTS AND DISCUSSION

The results are graphically summarized in Figure 5. Comparison of good and poor readers yielded no significant results, and the distinction was disregarded for subsequent comparisons.

Proximity. The only significant difference occurred at step 4, where a greater percentage of older subjects reproduced the lines as pairs than in the case of the younger group.

Closure. On all the other problems, nearly all our subjects eventually achieved the desired *Gestalt,* but on *Closure-Letter* task only 68 per cent of the total number of subjects recognized the letter "E." Perhaps this was due to the limited exposure time. The results also show that older subjects recognized the letter sooner and closed the geometrical figure sooner than did the younger ones. More of the sixteen-year-old deaf group recognized the letter than did the hearing subjects of the same age, while, for the geometrical figure, the younger deaf surpassed the hearing in drawing the *Gestalt.*

108

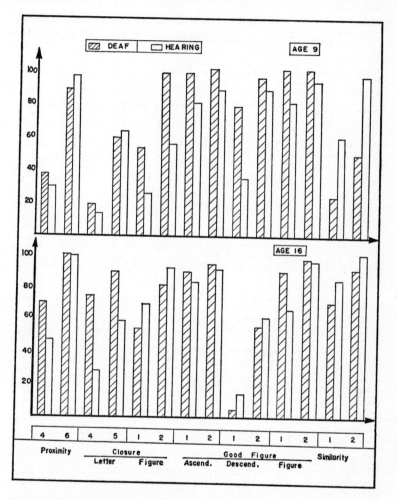

Figure 5. Percentage of subjects reproducing drawings according to Gestalt laws of organization at the indicated steps for each of the seven tasks.

109

Good Form.

1. Letter:

a. Ascending Series. The results suggest that perceptual performances were surprisingly equal. The general trend points to a closer adherence to *Gestalt* organization by the deaf, though no statistically meaningful differences were observed.

b. Descending Series. Step 1 refers to the least *Gestalt*-like figure presented. The 9-year-old deaf children persisted in their perception of the well-formed letter longer than did hearing children of that age, although by the end of the task they noticed the distortion as often as the hearing subjects did. The deaf did not differ significantly at the older age level. The combined older subjects, however, discriminated among the drawings sooner and more often than the younger.

2. Geometrical Figure. No significant differences were noted here among the groups. The trend was toward a greater discrepancy between the younger deaf and hearing, with the older groups showing equal ability to discriminate between the drawings.

Similarity. The reproduction of the pattern in this task was achieved sooner and more frequently by the older than by the younger group. The general difference favoring the hearing over the deaf group was due mainly to the performance of the younger deaf.

In summary, the linguistically deficient deaf differed from the hearing in three out of seven tasks. On the *Closure-Letter* task, they recognized an incomplete letter earlier than the hearing control group. The second notable difference was on the one task in which persistence, rather than achievement of the *Gestalt* principle was tested. Undoubtedly the four problems preceding this one established a behavioral "set" toward completion of the *Gestalt*. Perhaps the younger deaf children held to this "set" more strongly than did the hearing simply because deaf persons cannot be as certain as can the hearing about the meaning and instructions of any given problem situation. Moreover, the difference obtained in the final grouping, combining both age levels, may be seen to stem quite clearly from the performance of the younger deaf subjects.

Finally, on the figure-ground similarity problem, the younger deaf were less successful than the comparable hearing group. These results apparently agree with the findings of a similar study by Myklebust and Brutten (1953) with a similar age group. However, this study leads us to differ with the argument of these authors for a perceptual deficit in deaf children since we found that the younger deaf children had difficulty in understanding the instructions on this problem. Their difficulties were controlled but not completely overcome by the use of the sample figure. This task was the only one requiring a practice problem, indicating that it was especially hard to give adequate nonverbal instructions on this task. The older deaf group, on the other hand, appeared to the experimenter to grasp the instructions as well as the hearing group and subsequently performed on the same level as did the hearing group.

We should like to emphasize, in line with Werner's thinking, that on all perceptual tasks two tendencies may be observed: the principles of *Gestalt;* and the developmental principle of differentiation. These principles may work together on some tasks and against one another on other tasks. It is noteworthy that the two problems in which the younger deaf were inferior to the hearing children called primarily for a discriminatory rather than a global or *Gestalt* approach.

The only relatively pure problem for testing the operation of *Gestalt* principles was provided by the lines in the proximity series. All the other stimuli used in the various tasks presented an additional factor influencing recognition and reproduction in the form of potentially familiar and meaningful configurations. The results on the proximity task therefore strongly indicate a basic equality between deaf and hearing persons in perceptual *Gestalt* performance. If the general trend indicated anything specific, it was that the deaf subjects, both younger and older, perceived the pairing-off sooner than the others. Also, the results on the *Closure* task seem to point out that lack of verbal experience does not hinder the closure of these figures even though one was a highly verbal symbol.

These observations lead to the conclusion that language-deprived subjects, while showing no significant difference from the hearing groups, more consistently organize their percepts according to the principles of *Gestalt*. In accordance with the developmental theories of Werner and others, one may reason that this tendency on the part of the deaf shows their greater reliance on preverbal modes of perceptual organization. It is conceivable that a deaf subject's superior performance on certain problems may be due to his less sophisticated approach to the situation. In such cases, the hearing person's greater supply of available verbal mediators multiplies his possible choices and may actually hinder him in performing the task.

While emphasis on *Gestalt* organization or misunderstanding of instructions led the younger deaf to a faulty perception and reproduction of some figures which required breaking the totality of a pattern, the older subjects, regardless of language facility, performed on a comparable level. *Gestalt* organization, however, must not be considered simply as a preverbal or preadolescent type of perceptual approach. This becomes apparent by comparing the results obtained from the two age groups. On tasks illustrating two of the four *Gestalt* principles tested (proximity and closure), the older subjects succeeded better because they applied the *Gestalt* principle sooner and more often.

The most significant differences found were not by comparison of subjects with varying degrees of language experience, but rather by comparison of different ages or maturational levels. One may conclude therefore that age, or general nonverbal experience, is more important than specific language ability in its effect on tasks which are concerned with *Gestalt* laws of perception. In regard to the perceptual ability of the deaf, their reproduction of *Gestalt* forms in general gives little ground for the belief that they are basically different from the hearing.

CHAPTER IX

Piaget-Type Tasks

Piaget's theories of cognitive development, as will be more fully pointed out in Chapter XIII, appear to offer a particularly fruitful approach for the investigator concerned with the relation of thinking and language or the development of thinking in deaf persons. Although Piaget frequently uses verbal behavior as a criterion of intellectual functioning, he seems to postulate no consistent connection between language and thinking or at least the experimental tasks he employs are not formally "verbal" tasks.

Thus, a crucial question relates to the possibility of separating the linguistic from the nonlinguistic component in Piaget's tasks. Such an attempt has been undertaken successfully on a conceptual level by a number of scholars. On a practical level, however, it is quite difficult to dispense with language altogether, and an investigator is not likely to feel constrained to do this unless he is forced by the special circumstances of his subjects.

Such a special situation prevails when we study deaf people. As has been often pointed out in these pages, it is not reasonable to take even what we would regard as simple linguistic skill for granted. Certainly no hearing five-year-old child fails to comprehend the question, "Which has more?" and responds by pointing to the larger of two heaps of beans. With deaf children, well into the 12th or 13th year, it is quite difficult to replicate this situation. The younger ones will not have learned the word "more." In order to keep the question and answer situation, which is required in some Piaget-type experiments, one must have recourse to some sort of visual gestures. The following experiments will demonstrate more fully that this is not an easy problem, whether the experimenter has recourse to gestures, artificial or conventional sign language.

The conventional sign language of the deaf in America has a sign for "more." However, young deaf children are not familiar with the conventional sign language. Even when they begin to imitate others in making signs, they use these signs in a few natural situations among themselves and have little opportunity to use them on new occasions. Consequently, a sign meaning "more" would be used to indicate the desire for a bigger or a second helping at the table. If put before two heaps of unequal size, as often as not these children will point to the smaller one when given the signal "more."

We were at first surprised by this rather incongruous reaction until we realized that the signal "more" was understood by the deaf children in an opposite fashion from what we intended. We thought we had asked: "Which has or is more?" and apparently the deaf children understood: "Which needs more?" and replied sensibly to the latter interpretation of the question.

A problem of this sort is encountered in any observation regarding Piaget's principle of conservation, since it entails a judgmental reply of "same" or "different" regarding a certain aspect of reality. We wanted to know how deaf children judged amount of liquid and weight of an object when the visual configurations were changed. In testing the children, the experimenter poured liquid into differently shaped containers, or perhaps transformed a clay ball into a variety of shapes. Piaget observed that children below age six usually consider that a changing configuration implies a change in quantity or weight. Hence they do not "conserve" these aspects.

This problem had been attacked before. Oléron and Herren (1961) found, as expected, that deaf children were handicapped when verbal behavior was part of the experimental procedure. Consequently, they devised a series of three figures consisting of a scale pictured as leaning toward one or the other side or being in perfect balance. These pictures were to be equivalent symbols of the words "same weight," "heavy on one side," or "heavy on the other side" respectively. Testing children of various age groups, Oléron reported that deaf children appeared to be retarded as much as six years in comparison with the hearing group.

In the same study, Oléron reported a similar difference between deaf and hearing children in grasping the principle of quantity of a liquid. In his discussion, he admits that the figure of a six year lag need not be taken in an absolute sense, and that deaf children could have been handicapped in comparison with hearing children by some extraneous factor. Nevertheless, Oléron believed that Piaget's theory does not sufficiently emphasize the role of language in the development of cognitive behavior, and that his own study supports a stronger contribution of language. The following two studies are modified replications of Oléron's study. Some modifications were dictated by the belief that in spite of Oléron's precautions and pretraining, the use of pictorial symbols introduced a new difficulty which was mainly responsible for the results. Accordingly, these studies attempted to make use of a more natural nonverbal symbol for the crucial concepts of "same," "heavier," and "more."

116

The first experiment in this section concerns conservation of weight, while the second reports an investigation of conservation of quantity.

Experiment 7: Conservation of Weight
(Furth, 1964a)

SUBJECTS AND PROCEDURE

Twenty-two deaf children, the entire population of eight-year-old children in a state school for the deaf, were tested. Of these, 14 subjects came from classes which were considered average, the rest from three classes designated as slow. A hearing control group was selected from an elementary school located in a lower middle-class suburban neighborhood. First, a group of comparable age to the deaf was chosen, eight-year-old pupils from second grade. Since the first ten subjects performed considerably better than the deaf, with nine successes and only one failure, it was decided to test six-year-old first graders.

In this study, deaf and hearing children first judged the weight of two similar-looking clay balls to be equal. Then the shape of one of the balls was changed and they were asked again to indicate which one was heavier or whether both were of equal weight. Since deaf children, particularly at an early age level, are quite unable to comprehend a verbal sequence expressing that question, a training procedure with obviously different weights was devised, as well as a manual response.

The experimenter facing the child put an 8 oz. weight in the palm of each hand and moved both hands in a horizontal fashion, then encouraging the child to imitate this movement. Immediately afterward, one 8 oz. weight was exchanged for a 4 oz. weight, and the experimenter, taking a weight in each hand, lowered the hand with the heavier weight. He then ex-

117

changed the weights and consequently lowered the other hand. The child was then told to imitate the experimenter in his gestures of same weight (horizontal motion) and heavier (downward motion). Such gestures were thought to be relatively easy to grasp and to approximate the naturalness of language. Subsequently, 1 oz. and 16 oz. weights were introduced and after a minimum of six correct trials, the second stage of the pre-experimental procedure followed.

The child was shown three balls of clay, two alike and one obviously smaller. With these weights the child was encouraged to continue as before and to disregard any fine weight discrimination. After success without hesitation on six consecutive trials, the small clay ball was removed and the experimental series began.

The experimental series provided thirteen steps. In each step, two objects were handed to the child and he was expected to respond with one of the three weight responses. Transformation or division of one object into other shapes was done on the table, with the child watching the experimenter. The following list describes which object-shapes were put into the hands of the child on each step.

Step 1: Two similar balls.
Step 2: One ball —one snake.
Step 3: Half a ball — one snake.
Step 4: Two similar balls.
Step 5: One ball — two halves of the other ball.
Step 6: One ball — one half ball.
Step 7: Two similar balls.
Step 8: One ball — one ring.
Step 9: One disc — one ring.
Step 10: Half disc — half ring.
Step 11: Half disc and half ring in both hands.
Step 12: One ball — half ring.
Step 13: Two similar balls.

Steps 1, 4, 7, and 13 were base trials with similar objects, while steps 3, 6, and 12 constituted easy control trials, where a "same" response indicated failure to follow instructions. The critical trials for the principle of weight conservation were steps 2, 8, and 9. The division steps 5, 10, and 11 were introduced for further control and variety and gave those children who might be hesitant about the procedure an opportunity to correct themselves.

No corrections were given, but as many children hesitated or corrected themselves, second trials were given after the whole series was completed. A child was considered to have demonstrated conservation of weight if he gave correct responses to the three critical trials.

RESULTS AND DISCUSSION

The results indicated that the performance of these deaf children with a mean age of 8–5 was similar to that of hearing first graders with a mean age of 6–10. Table 9 summarizes an attempt to categorize performance according to degree of failure or success. "Hesitant" refers to subjects who had inconsistent responses on critical steps and often changed a response already made. These subjects performed second trials and were classified as failure or success depending on final performance.

Table 9—Number of Deaf and Hearing Children, Successful or Failing on Conservation of Weight

Performance	Deaf, Age 8	Hearing, Age 6	Hearing, Age 8
Failure			
Pre-test failure	1	2	0
Control failure	1	1	0
Clear failure	4	7	1
Hesitant failure	6	1	0
Success			
Hesitant corrected success	3	3	0
Self corrected success	5	3	2
Clear success	2	2	7
Total per cent success	45.4	41.1	90

Concerning the lower performance level of the deaf children, four points are to be noted. First, Oléron's reported discrepancy of six years was here reduced to 1 year and 7 months. Secondly, the hearing children's ceiling or near ceiling level was also considerably lowered and brought close to the age level of 7 suggested by Piaget. This gives some assurance that the results may represent a true picture of conceptual development. Moreover, the relatively large number of Hesitant Failures in the deaf is noteworthy. One can suggest that these six subjects gave objective indication of an unstable internal state. Finally, if one excludes those deaf pupils who came from slow classes, the difference between the eight-year-old hearing and deaf groups is no longer large enough to reach an acceptable significance level.

Can one relegate the eight children from the slow classes to the category of retarded children? This proportion would appear unusually large. Perhaps they exemplify a rather typical phenomenon in young deaf children. I refer here to early experiential deficiency, a blending of social, emotional, and intellective neglect, which is frequently observed in the deaf. Interestingly, the same children who were underdeveloped in conceptual conservation, tended to be the ones whom the school regarded as slow learners. When it is stated that the other deaf were in average classes, the reader should not think that such children had some notable linguistic competence. The next conservation study to be performed demonstrated that many deaf children who were six years older, still did not comprehend the question: "Which is more?"

That past experience as informal exposure to the physical world or formal training in numerical reasoning contributes substantially to the manifestation of logical behavior on conservation tasks has been demonstrated by Lovell and Ogilview (1961) and Wohlwill and Lowe (1962). Taking this line of reasoning, one may well account for the somewhat slower intellectual maturation of the deaf as manifested in this study by the fact that deaf children generally have less formal training in numbers and less general experience of the physical world than hearing peers.

Experiment 8: Conservation of Amount of Liquid

The rationale for this conservation study is closely related to the preceding investigation and the purpose was to explore further the first manifestation of logical operations when the child indicates his realization that an amount of liquid does not change if it is poured from one vessel into another of a different shape.

PROCEDURE

First, a procedure had to be devised to provide reasonable assurance that the language-deficient child comprehended the basic question and responded according to the intent of the experiment. By means of two small heaps of beans of obviously unequal size, the experimenter trained each subject to point to the larger heap. As the relative size of the heaps was altered, the subject was instructed to avoid any fine discrimination and simply respond with the manual sign for "same" if the heaps appeared equal in size. At each trial, the experimenter asked "Which is more?" at the same time employing the conventional sign for "more." As was mentioned before, a number of deaf subjects misunderstood this question.

Two standard beakers were filled with different amounts of water behind a screen and placed before the child. After a correct answer to the question of the examiner, the amount of water was equalized, and the child was expected to respond with "same" to the standard question. Then, in step A, one of the beakers was placed on a wooden block and the standard question was asked. If the child pointed to the beaker on the block instead of indicating "same" he was corrected by the

121

examiner. In step B, the child was shown one standard beaker and one wide culture-dish, both filled with water to an equal height. The standard question was asked and the answer again corrected if necessary. Steps A and B were introduced in an attempt to train the child unambiguously that the question did not refer to the height of the water.

Experimental Trials. Each time the amount of water was changed, the standard question "Which glass has more water?" or "Which has more to drink?" was asked. To relieve the monotony, on other than criterion trials, the basic question was sometimes phrased: "Are they the same?" When a child gave a "same" response consistently, trials were interspersed where a "more" response was obviously correct, to control for perseveration in responding "same."

Step 1. After the child said "same" to the equal amounts of water in two standard beakers, a thin cylinder was introduced and water from the standard beaker poured into the cylinder. The standard question was asked and then the water was poured back again into the beaker.

Step 2. In this step the procedure was similar to step 1 except that a wide beaker was introduced.

Step 3. Two glass bottles closed on top were shown which contained the same amount of water when standing upright. After the child responded "same" to the standard question, one bottle was turned horizontally and the question was asked again.

Step 4. The child was shown a standard beaker filled with water about one-half in. higher than the wide beaker. The standard question was asked and if the child pointed to the standard beaker as having more water, some water was poured out from this beaker and the question asked again. This procedure was repeated until the child pointed to the wide beaker as having more water. Then the procedure was reversed, and the water was added to observe the point at which the child would reverse his judgment.

Steps 1 to 3 were repeated to observe possible changes and at times more questions were added in order to ascertain hearing children's own verbalization when it was feasible. These questions were of the following kind: "How do you know?" or "Why is there more in this than in that?" Steps 1 and 2 were criterion trials.

RESULTS AND DISCUSSION

Prepared with the foregoing procedure, we expected somewhat similar results as had obtained on conservation of weight tasks. However, as we worked with a specially selected group of deaf children between the ages of 8 and 10 and could not get through to them on the pre-experimental procedure, with one solitary exception, we turned to an older age group. With twenty subjects in the 12 to 14 group, we obtained about 43 per cent success. With an older age group, from 16 onward, success was general and so clear that the experimenter could observe attitudes and gestures indicating surprise that these subjects should be exposed to such childish tricks.

Table 10 indicates a classification of the performance of hearing and deaf children on these tasks. We started with hearing children in Grade 3, as Bruner (1964) had indicated on a similar procedure almost 100 per cent success at age 9. In our case 70 per cent of the nine-to-ten-year-old children gave logically adequate replies, and in Grade 5, the high level of 95 per cent success was reached.

According to these results, deaf children would be five years late in grasping a logical principle which, like conservation of quantity, is postulated to be emerging in the beginning of the concrete operational stage. In Oléron's procedure, not more than 50 per cent of the deaf succeeded even above age 16 and at the age of 13-14 when 43 per cent of the deaf in our study succeeded, the corresponding percentage for Oléron was only 20 per cent. A similar difference is noted with the

123

Table 10—Number of Failing and Successful Subjects in Various Groups on Conservation of Quantity of Liquid

	HEARING		DEAF			RURAL *	
	9–10	11–12	10 and Under	12–14	16 and Over	9–10	13–14
Failure**							
Consistent	—	—	3†	2	—	4	—
Inconsistent	—	—	—	4	—	4	—
Hesitant	3	—	—	3	—	2	—
Partial	3	1	—	2	—	—	—
Success††							
Corrected	1	3	—	4	—	3	1
Clear	13	16	1	5	7	5	19
Percentage Success							
This study	70	95	7	45	100	44	100
Oléron and Herren	31	62	0	20	50	—	—

* The performance of this group is discussed in Chapter XI.
** Failure is defined as nonconservation responses on both criterion trials. Consistent = height dimension regarded consistently. Inconsistent = height or width dimension regarded. Hesitant = indication of initial conservation response. Partial = consistent conservation response on one criterion trial.
† Of 15 selected subjects in this group eleven failed in the pre-experimental instructions and thus cannot be classified in this table.
†† Success is defined as final conservation response on both criterion trials. Corrected = some initial non-conservation.

hearing. While only 31 per cent of children at age 9-10 succeed according to Oléron, 70 per cent succeeded here.

There were thus substantial discrepancies in the behavioral manifestation of the supposedly common thinking operation of conservation. One can compare the five-year lag of the present experiment in conservation of volume with the one-year lag of the previous study in conservation of weight. Additionally, there are the results of these two studies in which at least all the 16-year-old deaf succeeded, and Oléron's findings of barely 50 per cent success at a comparable age level. To these may be added differences in successful performance of hearing subjects, as reported here, by Oléron and elsewhere in the literature. Such age differences cannot be simply dismissed as minor variations. Quite clearly then, the particular testing procedure through which logical thinking is observed affects the results strongly so that the basic aim of the observation is overshadowed.

CHAPTER X

Logical Classification

In the experiments covered so far, developmental stages in deaf persons were observed and references were made to the likelihood that behavioral differences due to special environmental and educational circumstances may no longer be manifest at an adult level. It would seem particularly important, therefore, to test deaf adults who have left school and live an average life of a deaf adult in our society. These deaf adults, after all, illustrate the end product of development, and the eventual functioning of adult intelligence is the critical concern not only of the educator but also of the developmental psychologist.

A preliminary investigation was carried out with deaf students at Gallaudet College, with the explicit understanding that these were not typical deaf adults. On the contrary, they constituted the "cream of the crop," that small proportion of all deaf pupils who master linguistic skill sufficiently to enable them to pursue higher education.

Past research had suggested that a simple discovery type task yielded results that were too meager to serve as the basis for inferences regarding intellectual processes. This study accordingly used a transfer paradigm which would manifest the way in which a previously attained principle is utilized. Thus, we can attempt an answer not merely to the question: "Was a particular concept attained?" but to the question: "To what purpose or how well was it attained?"

Experiment 9: Classification Transfer *(Furth, 1963a)*

SUBJECTS AND PROCEDURE

Four classes of hearing college students were compared with four classes of deaf students at Gallaudet College, with each of the four classes arbitrarily assigned to one of four transfer conditions. A group procedure was used throughout. Task I, the attainment task, was identical for all conditions.

A set of 48 white cards was prepared on which were glued two geometric figures cut from colored construction paper. From six figures (circle, ellipse, crescent, square, rectangle, triangle) and six colors (black, blue, green, red, orange, yellow), two colored figures were systematically selected to exemplify twelve instances each of the following four separate classes: I. Form same, Color same (Fs, Cs); II. Form same, Color different (Fs, Cd); III. Form different, Color same (Fd, Cs); IV. Form different, Color different (Fd, Cd). See Figure 6 for a sample of the four stimulus classes.

These cards were presented as 48 stimuli to the groups, one at a time for five sec. each, in a systematic order. Each student had a response sheet on which he had to respond to the presented stimulus by writing down one of three letters of the alphabet. After all students had responded, the experimenter gave them the appropriate response, thus providing information and correction. For Task I, the letters *A B C* were arbitrarily assigned as follows: Any stimulus card belonging to class Fs, Cs or to the class Fs, Cd was associated with *A*,

126

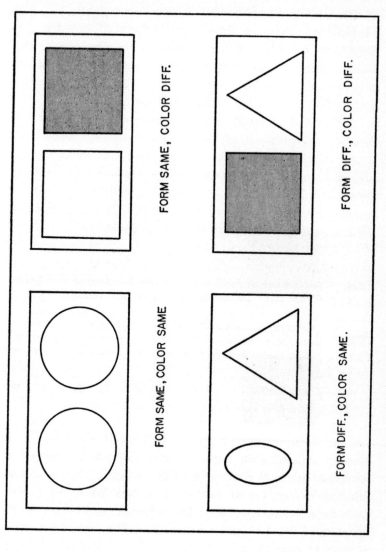

Figure 6. Sample of cards belonging to four different logical classes.

FORM SAME, COLOR DIFF.

FORM DIFF., COLOR DIFF.

FORM SAME, COLOR SAME

FORM DIFF., COLOR SAME.

127

while the class Fd, Cs was associated with *B,* and the class Fd, Cd with *C.*

Task I was the attainment or discovery task and, as Table 11 indicates and as a subsequent analysis of variance confirmed, no reliable differences between the groups emerged. Furthermore, on a criterion of nine correct choices in ten successive trials, only 10 students from a total of 131 hearing and 8 of 99 deaf students failed on Task I.

Task I was designed to make it possible for all subjects to discover the presence of four separate logical classes, even though they classified the stimulus instances of those four classes into only three response categories. To discover the presence of four classes, a person had to master the disjunctive (either/or) combination of two stimulus classes. That is, on Task I he had to recognize that he responded with one letter *A* to the two classes Fs, Cs or Fs, Cd.

Table 11—Number of Subjects, Combined Response Categories, and Mean Error on Attainment Task and Transfer Task

Transfer Condition	SUBJECTS		COMBINED RESPONSE CLASSES*		ATTAINMENT		TRANSFER	
	Hearing	Deaf	Attainment	Transfer	Hearing	Deaf	Hearing	Deaf
1	38	20	Fs Cs	Fd Cs and Fd Cd	10.5	12.9	3.2	11.7
2	39	25	and	Fs Cs and Fd Cs	8.4	11.1	2.7	9.3
3	40	26	Fs Cd	Fs Cd and Fd Cd	8.9	9.7	5.6	9.9
4	24	28		Fs Cd and Fd Cs	9.8	12.3	9.8	10.9

* F = Form; C = Color; s = same; d = different.

Immediately following Task I, Task II was given as a transfer task with the same stimulus material. A new set of response letters *Q R S* were to be associated with the four stimulus classes, but in a different manner from Task I. Subjects were divided into four different transfer conditions. An inspection of Table 11 indicates that Task II essentially involved a shift to new disjunctive combinations listed for the four transfer conditions.

128

RESULTS AND DISCUSSION

Insofar as the handling of disjunctive combinations has been demonstrated to be a relatively difficult task, one could expect that performance on Task II would be related to the manner in which Task I was performed. A clear grasp of the four separate classes and of the possible disjunctive combinations would argue for a level of concept attainment on Task I which is unaffected by the particular condition of the transfer task.

However, the results with the hearing summarized in Table 11 do not confirm such a state of affairs. On the contrary, the first and second transfer conditions were significantly easier than the third and the last, while the last was not only the most difficult shift but also the only condition in which the mean error score did not improve from Task I to Task II.

In searching for an explanation of the fact that hearing college students shifted in the stated order of difficulty, one must consider possible verbalizations which the students may have employed. The following list would express a possible and perfectly logical principle of sorting which does not, however, explicitly indicate the four basic classes and their disjunctive combinations:

Task I (All conditions): "If form same, disregard color."
Task II (Condition 1): "If form different, disregard color."
(Condition 2): "If color same, disregard form."
(Condition 3): "If color different, disregard form."
(Condition 4): "The combined class differs on one dimension only."

It should be apparent that with such an implicit or explicit grasp of principles, transfer in Condition 4 should be most difficult, as in fact it was. Condition 3 should come next, as it retained the general verbal outline of the principle but

129

changed two terms. Conditions 1 and 2 changed only one term and should be easiest. The obtained result corresponded to the reasoning implied by this verbalized principle.

Possibly the hearing students' behavior was controlled by a verbalized principle which disguised the conceptual disjunctive aspect of the classification behavior, but facilitated shift to those transfer conditions in which a similar sentence frame could be employed. For the fourth shift condition, however, the conceptual grasp of class attainment on Task I was the one facilitating circumstance. This facilitation is shown by the fact that a group of 28 students who were given this task without prior exposure to Task I obtained an average error score of 20.5. Thus on Transfer Condition 4, verbal habits were of no particular help, but prior performance on Task I was a facilitative influence. Consequently, one may regard performance on this Transfer Condition as an indicator of the level of performance on Task I, involving the conceptual mastery of the disjunctive response category.

While this reasoning is admittedly speculative, it is rather striking that the deaf students did not differ in transfer performance according to conditions, as did the hearing. They were poorer than the hearing on the three Transfer Conditions in which verbalization possibly helped the hearing. On the Fourth Condition, however, which indicated mastery or level of conceptual grasp, there was no difference between the hearing and deaf subjects.

Apparently, even the deaf college student was not so ready as his hearing peer to utilize verbal principles, a fact which should cause little surprise. One might expect that on verbal tasks these students stand midway between hearing persons who enjoy a readily available linguistic competence and the many deaf persons who have hardly any language ability. However, regarding concept level or attainment of a disjunctive class, as manifested in Transfer Condition 4, verbalization or lack of linguistic skill did not have any appreciable influence.

Experiment 10: Conceptual Performance in Deaf Adults (Furth, 1964b)

The previous study has shown how precarious our interpretation of data is, if one assumes that a subject will solve a given problem in the manner in which it was originally conceived by the investigator. Many subjects apparently did not conceive of the task as a disjunctive problem, and verbal formulation could have been of some advantage on certain of the shift conditions.

This study attempted to improve on the previous one by testing subjects individually and starting with separate training on each of two dimensions. The critical test for conceptual ability was a subsequent transfer situation in which these separate dimensions were combined to form increasingly complex sorting principles or concepts. The experimental operation of combining and logically relating given instances of classes could be assumed to be a mark of intelligent behavior and to sample a natural intellective process of the developing child.

SUBJECTS AND PROCEDURE

To make certain that this test was related to usual measures of intelligence, it was decided to give the entire procedure first to a normal sample of hearing adults who could be tested on their general intellectual ability as well. After it was observed that the test differentiated reliably between hearing persons with above and below average intelligence, and as the relation between success on this test and intelligence was now empirically established, it was given to a group of deaf

131

adults. Our interest was centered on the typical deaf adult, and consequently we excluded those who had been to college or who had not been functionally deaf from earliest childhood. The final comparison was made on a sample of 30 hearing and 30 deaf persons, all falling within the age range of 20 to 50.

The material of the *Color-Form* task (CF) as described in the previous study was employed in five different conditions. On CF_1 a subject had to sort the deck of 48 cards into two boxes. The sorting principle to be discovered was: Color same (Cs) into one box; Color different (Cd) into the other box. A rather strict objective criterion of ten consecutive correct choices was used. If necessary, after 48 trials, additional non-verbal help was given by pointing, so that all subjects eventually passed the criterion. Similar help was also given on subsequent tasks, if necessary, so as to have reasonable assurance that a subject had mastered the concept of the previous task before going on to the next.

For CF_2 the subject had to shift the principle of sorting to: Form same (Fs) into one box, Form different (Fd) into the other box. After the subjects had been exposed to the four separate classes Fs, Fd, Cs, Cd, two other CF tasks followed in which these classes were differently combined. For CF_3 three response boxes were used and a subject had to combine the above classes into the following three response categories: Fd, Cs into box 1; Fd, Cd into box 2; Fs, Cs or Fs, Cd into box 3. This task was actually identical with Task I of the previous study except that CF_1 and CF_2 preceded here with exposure to the simple classes. Consequently, performance on CF_3 would seem to be a critical test of the ability to use and combine previously acquired logical classes.

CF_4 followed with a shift to a different combination of classes, viz., Fs, Cs into box 1, Fs, Cd or Fd, Cs into box 2, and Fd, Cd into box 3. This shift, identical to the Transfer Condition 4 in the previous experiment, had been shown to be the one least facilitated by verbal habits and related to conceptual grasp of the separate classes.

A fifth *Color-Form* task, CF_5, required a shift to a new aspect of the stimulus cards. The three new sorting principles associated with the previously disregarded dimension of curvature, were: "Both figures irregular; Both figures round; One figure angular, the other round." CF_5 exemplified the kind of shift in which the deaf at times were found to be inferior to hearing controls. The difficulty of this shift is evident as the preceding series of CF tests may have generated a set to concentrate on the dimensions of color or form which now, in CF_5, had become dimensions to be disregarded.

An additional *Direction* task (D) was interpolated between CF_1 and CF_3 for the purpose of breaking the monotony of working five times with identical materials, and also to afford some additional training on a less structured task and on the principle of disjunctive sorting. D_1 consisted of a deck of 40 cards with different linear figures drawn in black ink. These drawings were easily recognized as occurring in one of two directions: Vertical (V) or Slanted right (Sl_r). For D_1 a subject had to discover these sorting principles of direction on the basis of 20 V cards and 20 Sl_r cards. In D_2 40 new stimulus cards were added to the set of cards, 20 of the new stimuli represented the class Horizontal (H) and 20 the class Slanted left (Sl_l). The task was to sort the deck into the following three response categories: V; H; Sl (regardless of direction). Immediately following D_2 came D_3, in which Sl had to be broken up into Sl_r and Sl_l, as the subject was now required to combine V and Sl_r into one disjunctive response category, leaving Sl_l and H as the two other categories.

RESULTS AND DISCUSSION

Table 12 provides a summary of the entire battery of tasks, the order in which they were presented, and the results in terms of number of subjects reaching criterion without the

133

experimenter's help on a particular task. It is apparent that differences between hearing and deaf were rather small except on D_3 where a significantly higher proportion of hearing subjects succeeded. A similar picture emerged when Errors or Trials to criterion were analyzed as average performance measures.

Table 12—Order, Kind of Tasks, and Number of Successful Subjects

Task		Response Classes*	SUCCESS† Hearing	Deaf
CF_1	Discovery in a structured task	Cs; Cd.	13	12
D_1	Discovery in an unstructured task	V; Sl_r.	18	13
CF_2	Shift to a previously irrelevant dimension	Fs; Fd.	22	19
D_2	Addition of a new value to old dimension	V; Sl; H.	29	25
D_3	Break up a class to form disjunction	V or Sl_r; Sl_l; H.	20	11
CF_3	Combine familiar elements into conjunction and disjunction	Fs Cs or Fs Cd; Fd Cs; Fd Cd.	20	19
CF_4	Shift to a different disjunction	Fs Cd or Fd Cs; Fs Cs; Fd Cd.	21	19
CF_5	Shift to a new aspect within familiar dimension	Angular; Round; Angular and Round.	14	14

* C = Color, F = Form, s = same, d = different. V = Vertical, H = Horizontal, Sl = Slanted, r = right, l = left.
† Based on 30 subjects in each group.

These global results can be discussed under various aspects. For conceptual discovery, the deaf were apparently equal to the hearing on CF_1 but were possibly somewhat poorer on D_1. Shifting from form to color on CF_2 was accomplished with equal success for both groups. Concerning shift performance, the lack of differences on CF_5, the last task, is particularly notable in view of the rigidity which the deaf at times exhibit. The fact that the deaf were less inhibited in shifting may be related to various conditions: the training procedure built into the task, the eventual success they achieved on each task, or possibly the general experience of adult living which made the deaf more flexible and prepared to face new viewpoints.

The deaf person's relative failure on D_3 could be associated with the discovery aspect of this task or with the first occurrence of a disjunctive sorting principle. One may also speculate that the "concrete" manual sign for "slanted"—a slanted position of the arm regardless of direction—may make it harder for the deaf to discover the break-down of the category "Slanted" into "Slanted left" and "Slanted right."

However, the most important results concern the critical tasks CF_3 and CF_4, in which the previously discovered elements of color and form were conjunctively and disjunctively combined and then regrouped in a different manner of disjunction. A consistently lower performance of deaf subjects on these two tasks could have suggested that deaf adults suffer some permanent conceptual deficiency in the use and comprehension of logical classes and combinations. However, the observed similarity in performance level was quite striking. If further experiments provide similar evidence, these results should have far-reaching implications for our view on the intelligence of deaf adults. The following investigation was carried out to provide additional empirical evidence.

Experiment 11: Logical Symbol Discovery and Use (Furth and Youniss, 1965)

A series of three studies fall under this heading, but only those two which employed deaf and hearing subjects are reported here. The first one, Symbol Discovery, was designed for a younger age group. The other, Symbol Use, was thought suitable for adults. For reasons that will become clear in the course of explaining the obtained results, we gave these same tasks to a rural hearing sample. A description of this third part is in Chapter XI.

The previous studies in this section with deaf adults used conceptual tasks from which some logical operations could be inferred. The Classification Shift experiment left some doubt

135

as to how subjects actually operated. The training procedure of the Conceptual Performance experiment made it possible to relate success on CF_3 and CF_4 to grasp of classes and their possible groupings. Here we intended to go one step further by employing the kind of symbolic problems which by any kind of definition relate to "abstract" thinking. Our first task was to devise a procedure which required no connected verbal language. As usual, we first obtained some normative data with hearing controls before giving the tasks to the deaf.

SYMBOL DISCOVERY

Subjects and Procedure. This task used a group procedure and consisted of an *Attainment* and *Tranfer* task. Its purpose was to investigate whether grade school children could by trial and correction learn the significance of three elementary logical connectives: · symbol for "and" or Conjunction; ‾ symbol for "not" or Negation; / symbol for "either-or, one but not the other," or Exclusive disjunction. For *Attainment,* the subjects were instructed to write one of the three letter combinations: $B \cdot R$; B / R; $\overline{B} \cdot \overline{R}$ as a response to the presentation of a series of 48 cards with color combinations. Through a correction procedure the subjects learned to associate the response $B \cdot R$ to cards which showed Blue and Red; the response B / R to cards which had one of the four color combinations: Red and Yellow, Red and Green, Blue and Yellow, Blue and Green; and finally the response $\overline{B} \cdot \overline{R}$ when the color combination Yellow and Green was shown. The three possible responses were constantly in sight of the subjects and the examiner indicated that B referred to Blue, and R to Red, but no mention was made concerning the logical symbols · , / , ‾ ·

Immediately following the first task, the subjects had a *Transfer* task with one of three possible response choices: $C \cdot D$, C / D, $\overline{C} \cdot \overline{D}$. The examiner first pointed out that C referred to Circular or Round, and D referred to Dark Color.

136

There were 18 presentations of a stimulus card, 5 cards with dark purple circular figures, 5 with light yellow angular figures, and the rest divided between purple angular and yellow circular.

RESULTS AND DISCUSSION

This task when given to 309 children in Grades 4 through 7 yielded the following interesting results: On *Attainment,* an equal proportion of about 45 per cent of the children in each grade reached a criterion on ten consecutive correct choices, but on *Transfer* a sharp break emerged between the successful subjects in the older and the younger groups, with only 11 per cent of the younger against 64 per cent of the older performing better than on a chance level.

These results, spelled out in greater detail in Youniss and Furth (1964), suggest that the majority of the older children who learned the correct associations on *Attainment,* learned them in a meaningful manner. That is, they discovered the significance of the logical connectives and subsequently could transfer their use to a new stimulus situation in which no correction or feedback was given. The younger children, however, although they learned the association on *Attainment,* either learned the relation between the logical connectives and their responses so poorly that they could not re-apply them in *Transfer,* or, more likely, they did not pay much attention to the possible meaning of the lines or dots.

The discrepancy between the two age groups may be related to the intellectual initiative with which the learning task of *Attainment* was approached. This was essentially a rote learning task in which children could learn to give the correct response from memory with a minimum of reasoning. But the task became one of logical comprehension for those older subjects who looked for and discovered the significance of the logical connectives. This first task, by itself, failed to give any

137

clues concerning the intellectual curiosity with which a subject learned to make right responses. But performance on *Transfer* appeared to be a direct function of possessing a sufficient degree of intellectual curiosity on the *Attainment* task to discover the meaning of the logical symbols.

When this task was given to a group of 27 deaf children, comparable in age to pupils in Grades 6 and 7, we observed that of those 15 subjects who reached criterion on *Attainment* (a proportion of success similar to that achieved by the hearing), not a single one succeeded on *Transfer*. Would an older age group of deaf persons, we wondered, exhibit a greater degree of intellectual initiative? Forty seniors, aged 16 to 20, cooperated and 65 per cent reached criterion on *Attainment*. However, *Transfer* performance of these 26 successful subjects indicated rather clearly that the vast majority of deaf seniors had succeeded on *Attainment* by rote, not by reason: only 3 subjects performed better than chance on *Transfer*.

The question naturally arises: Is it that the deaf are simply not curious enough to look for rational rules in their choice behavior, preferring rather to carry on by rote? Or is the comprehension and use of logical symbols beyond their ken? It was to give an answer to these rather crucial questions and to sample again in a new manner the conceptual performance of deaf adults that the following study was devised.

LOGICAL SYMBOL USE

Subjects and Procedure. This task is a modification of what is called truth tables in elementary books of logic. Its purpose was to train subjects in the meaning and use of the three logical connectives for conjunction ($\cdot$), disjunction (/) and negation ($^{-}$). The only other symbols were a black circle or triangle referring to Circle and Triangle respectively and a small square, pencilled in blue or red, referring to the respective colors. These symbols are indicated here by the letters C, T,

B, R. There were two parts to this task, each consisting of 3 sub-tasks. The first part employed the symbols B, R, $\overline{B}$, $\overline{R}$, $B \cdot R$, B / R. The second part added these symbols: $B \cdot \overline{R}$, $\overline{B} \cdot R$, $\overline{B} \cdot \overline{R}$, $B \overline{\cdot} R$, $B \overline{/} R$.

The subject's task was to comprehend the meaning of the logical symbols and apply them to concrete instances. When symbol cards were matched against instances, the subject had to indicate whether or not the instance belonged to the symbol. As an illustration, with the instance showing the colors blue and yellow, he had to accept the following symbol cards: B, $\overline{R}$, B / R, $B \cdot \overline{R}$, $B \overline{\cdot} R$, while rejecting the rest of the symbols as not agreeing with the instance: R, $\overline{B}$, $B \cdot R$, $\overline{B} \cdot R$, $B \overline{/} R$. Here we matched one instance against each one of a number of symbolized classes. We could also take one symbol and match it against each of six given instances. Thus the symbol $C \cdot \overline{T}$ (meaning the concept of the presence of a circle combined with the absence of a triangle) is positively illustrated by instance cards showing circle, or circle and crescent, but the answer "no" is correct when the symbol card $C \cdot \overline{T}$ is matched against instance cards showing: circle and triangle; triangle; rectangle and triangle; rectangle.

Color and *Form* alternated on this task, with half the subjects starting with *Color,* continuing on *Form* for sub-tasks III to V and switching back to *Form* on VI while the other half started with *Form* and switched dimensions on III and VI. As the former study with youngsters and a pilot study with adults showed that a sizeable proportion of over 50 per cent never learned comprehension of the logical symbols through discovery, and as our main concern was with transfer or use of the logical symbols, we decided to minimize the discovery aspect. Each subject was told through words or gestures what the first six logical symbol cards referred to. Thus it was pointed out to the subject that C stood for Circle, T for Triangle, that the line over C meant "not" (negation), hence $\overline{C}$ stood for "not Circle," that the dot between $C \cdot T$ meant "and"

139

(conjunction), and that the slanted line meant "or" in the sense of "one of two but not both" (exclusive disjunction).

After subjects had rehearsed these instructions, no further help or verbalizations were permitted and sub-task I began. Six color instances (blue, black, red and blue, red, blue and yellow, green and red) were laid out and the first symbol card (B) was placed above each of the six instances. At each match the subject responded with "yes" or "no" and was corrected if necessary. Subsequently the second to the sixth symbol card ($R, \overline{B}, \overline{R}, B \cdot R, B / R$) was matched against each instance.

Sub-task II differed from I only in that all symbol cards were first laid out before the subject, and each instance, one at a time, was matched against each of the symbols. For sub-task III, the experimenter switched dimensions to form but otherwise no new logical condition was introduced. This critical task had three trials for each of the following six logical operations or conditions:

1) Negation (e.g., Symbol $\overline{C}$);
2) Conjunction ($C \cdot R$);
3) Simplification (C matched against Circle *and* another form);
4) "Simple" Disjunction (C / T matched against Circle alone);
5) "Exclusive" Disjunction (C / T against Circle *and* Triangle; correct response "no");
6) Disjunction with "Addition" (C / T against Circle *and* any other form except triangle).

Sub-tasks IV and V employed the procedure and instance cards of tasks I and II except that the following five new symbols were used:

7) $C \cdot \overline{T}$ and $\overline{C} \cdot T$ (Conjunction with one Negation);
8) $\overline{C} \cdot \overline{T}$ (Conjunction with two Negations);
9) $\overline{C \cdot T}$ (Negation of Conjunction);
10) $\overline{C / T}$ (Negation of Disjunction); together with C / T (Exclusive Disjunction as above).

Sub-task VI had three trials of each of the above five logical operations, but symbols and instances changed back from Form to Color. Figure 7 illustrates a specific symbol, an instance and the correct response for each of the ten logical conditions.

RESULTS AND DISCUSSION

These *Symbol Use* tasks were given first to a sample of 26 enlisted men as normative controls. The results as tabulated in the first two rows of Table 13 demonstrate that these logical operations satisfactorily differentiated the high from the low intelligence group and that, as expected, errors increased as a function of complexity of concept and interfering perceptual pull of the instance.

Table 13—Mean Error of Control, Deaf and Rural Subjects on Symbol Use for Each Logical Operation
(Maximum error score for each operation = 3)

Task III

Group	Negation	Conjunction	Simplification	DISJUNCTION			Total
				Simple	Exclusive	Addition	
Control							
High	.23	.19	.54	.31	1.31	.69	3.27
Low	.69	1.02	.62	.88	1.69	1.46	6.36
Combined	.46	.60	.58	.59	1.50	1.08	4.81
Deaf	.25	.55	.35	.40	1.80	.85	4.20
Rural	.40	.75	.55	.45	1.70	.80	4.65

Tasks IV, V and VI Combined

Group	Exclusive Disjunction	CONJUNCTION WITH		NEGATED		Total
		One Negation	Two Negations	Conjunction	Disjunction	
Control						
High	.53	.50	.42	1.06	1.41	3.91
Low	1.10	.76	.91	1.22	1.28	5.27
Combined	.81	.63	.67	1.14	1.35	4.60
Deaf	.78	.57	.51	1.15	1.22	4.20
Rural	.92	.56	.69	1.28	1.19	4.64

The task was then administered to 20 deaf high school seniors, randomly selected from the group which had failed

OPERATION	SYMBOL	INSTANCE	RESPONSE
Negation	$\overline{O}$	■●	—
Conjunction	O·Δ	▲	—
Simplification	Δ	■▲	+
Disjunction "Simple"	O/Δ	▲	+
Disjunction "Exclusive"	O/Δ	▲●	—
Disjunction "Addition"	O/Δ	▲■	+
Conjunction (I Negation)	$\overline{O}$·Δ	▲	+
Conjunction (2 Negations)	$\overline{Δ}$·$\overline{O}$	●	—
Negated Conjunction	$\overline{Δ·O}$	▲	+
Negated Disjunction	$O\overline{7}Δ$	■	✝

Figure 7. Sample of symbol, instance and response for ten types of logical operations.

so conspicuously on *Symbol Discovery* some time before, and the results were compared against the combined results of the control group in rows 3 and 4. It becomes clear at once that the performance of the deaf and of the controls was quite similar. Such a similarity is a striking confirmation of the previous study which indicated that the deaf adult is as capable as any hearing person of comprehending and using logical operations. It also answers the crucial question about the reason for the deaf person's failure on *Symbol Discovery*. The performance of the deaf here gives evidence that comprehension and use of logical symbols is well within the capacity of such persons.

Specific failures in a number of test situations in which linguistic competence should not seem to be a priori a critical factor must somehow be accounted for as this converging series of studies implies a basic similarity in the thinking of the deaf and the hearing. It is the purpose of the next chapter to throw some light on these points and summarize the functioning of the intelligence of the deaf on the basis of the experimental evidence reported thus far.

CHAPTER XI

The Thinking of the Deaf

It is a scientific truism that the null hypothesis can, strictly speaking, never be tested or confirmed. If some of our experimental procedures do not yield the expected differences between deaf and hearing persons, one is still free to withhold judgment and consider the case not yet proven. Perhaps some better experimental methods and more powerful statistical techniques could show differences and support the general theory that linguistic deficiency is associated with inferior performance on intellectual tasks.

For those who wish to make a point in favor of this theoretical position, it is of course easy enough to single out some studies of thinking where the deaf trail behind the hearing. We mentioned in a previous chapter that more often than not the statement that the deaf are poor in concept formation or in abstract thinking was illustrated by the fact that they were severely retarded in linguistic behavior and the implication was that conceptual or abstract thinking *is* thinking expressed in verbal terms. Such reasoning is a patent misuse of an operational definition. It is one thing to denote the term "abstract thinking" by the term "verbal thinking." It is, however, quite another thing then to turn around and explain abstract thinking as being causally related to linguistic skill.

Leaving these verbal studies aside, we turn to a sizeable number of nonverbal investigations where the performance of deaf persons has been inferior to that of the hearing. Is there any consistent pattern, and can we state some reasonable conclusions about the intellectual functioning of the deaf on the basis of experimental evidence? Looking back on Chapters VII–X and taking account of some additional material, we are impressed with the fact that in no area of intellectual functioning do we find consistent results. The only possible exception is the area of verbal mediation where, curiously enough, the deaf perform in a manner consistently similar to the hearing, and on Piaget's tasks in which deaf children are uniformly retarded but eventually reach a mature level of response. On discovery and on shift tasks, the deaf are at times behind, but frequently they are not different from the hearing. On rote learning, in visual perception and immediate memory, there are no notable differences between the deaf and the hearing, nor did the deaf perform below the hearing on logical classifications and use of logical symbols.

Results showing no differences as for instance in the area of mediation, do not reveal much about the deaf, although they are of critical concern to psychological theories according to which differences could be expected. We shall return to this point later on.

I believe that the pattern of relative failure and success on the part of the deaf is inconsistent with any psychological explanation linking deafness or linguistic deficiency directly to the thinking process. There are now too many studies where the same deaf children have succeeded on one, but not on another task, whereas any general influence would have predicted failure on both tasks.

It seems then that the intellectual deficiency of deaf people, where it does exist, is associated with some specific situations which our investigations are beginning to highlight. The deaf are often insecure in an unstructured situation of intellectual discovery and are accordingly slow in seeing what may be more readily obvious to the hearing peer. I have not found that the deaf were incapable of understanding or of applying a principle as well as the hearing, once it was understood. But in some cases the deaf find it hard to discover the basis or reason for thinking.

In this connection let us compare the results of three studies reported in preceding chapters: *Part-Whole, Sameness-Opposite, Similarities*. In the first study the deaf were equal to the hearing. In the second the deaf were equal on *Sameness* and *Symmetry* to the hearing but inferior to them on *Opposite*. Finally, on *Similarities* the younger deaf were inferior, but the older ones were equal to the hearing control group. In all three studies there was a discovery aspect and it was most marked in *Similarities* in which each item required a new discovery. On this task the younger deaf subjects showed a slight retardation. In pointing to pictures which exemplified a concept-to-be-discovered, the deaf were on the whole somewhat less successful than the hearing. On the *Part-Whole* task, on the other hand, the discovery aspect was less pronounced. Instead, what we called "conceptual control," i.e., consistent behavior controlled by the once-discovered principle, was crucial. In *Sameness* and *Symmetry*, there was discovery of one concept only and here also the deaf were not inferior, except in the case of *Opposite* where we postulated a peculiar facilitation through linguistic usage. These studies illustrate the special conditions in which the deaf are sometimes inferior, particularly the younger deaf. This is in the area of discovery of a concept rather than comprehension or use of the concept.

This difficulty in discovering a principle is again clearly observed in the study of *Logical Symbol Discovery*. The deaf learned associations by rote and never bothered to look for reasons behind the symbols. Consequently they could not use these symbols in any other situations, while hearing controls quite readily comprehended the meaning of the symbols. We recall, however, that these same deaf young adults who discovered no generalized meaning in those symbols during the rote learning task could use and transfer them to new situations as readily as hearing persons once they were given the meaning of the symbols. Here again, on a task using a discovery principle the deaf lagged behind, but on a task requiring comprehension and use of a principle they were equal to the hearing.

Finally, on a number of Piaget-type studies, the deaf were at times markedly retarded and the question arises whether this result is due to their lack of conceptual comprehension or is perhaps again related to their difficulty in dealing with aspects of discovery and lack of initiative in reasoning. It is a precarious undertaking to analyze specific causes of failure on these tasks. We described in Chapter X how hard it was for deaf persons to interpret correctly such a simple question as "Which is more?" even when manual signs were employed. Moreover, there is usually a certain trick involved by the very fact that the examiner asks "Which is more?" when in fact the correct reply is "Neither. They are the same." Also, there is a way in which an objectively wrong answer may be subjectively correct, as could be pointed out in connection with the clay ball of greater density than an elongated stick. The ball definitely "feels" heavier than the stick even though the weight may be known to be the same.

The deaf have often been called "rigid" with regard to their thinking. Their inability or slowness in shifting from one principle or viewpoint to another has frequently been noted. Such slowness in shifting has been linked to the linguistic deficiency of the deaf and some resultant "concrete" attitude which is supposed to be related to or accounted for by a common source. Shifting is of course closely related to discovery of new conceptual aspects. Anyone who has observed the education of the deaf would not be surprised to see deaf children repeatedly sticking to a choice once declared correct, for they learn very early to repeat and repeat, in exact, parrot-like fashion. The attitude of repeating what has once been learned is drilled into them. The two transfer studies with deaf adults employed a training procedure for shifting and showed that shifting presented no special problem. It appeared that the training had implicitly taught them that shifting was permitted and encouraged.

As these are the main areas in which the deaf were found to be inferior, can one conceivably link this inferiority directly to linguistic deficiency? If language is the key factor, how does language facilitate discovery of new concepts while lack of it does not impede comprehension and use of concepts? This poses a further difficulty since conceptual comprehension and use appear to be purer aspects of intelligence than discovery. Why then should language affect a less and not affect a more important part of intelligence?

This dilemma epitomizes the condition of the serious investigator who examines the results of studies with the deaf and, knowing the linguistic deficiency of deaf persons, wants to generalize from the results to the linguistic deficiency. This linguistic deficiency is general. The very limited language laboriously assimilated by the deaf cannot reasonably be put on the lower end of a continuum, the other end of which is represented by the linguistic affluence of the hearing.

We should consider some additional points. Granted that the younger deaf child fails to give a logical answer to Piaget's tasks, how is it that the adolescent, still linguistically deficient, succeeds in these tasks easily? Or we may examine a number of studies in which the young deaf were just one or two years behind. In Alternation behavior, see p. 162, the five- and six-year-old deaf were about one year behind the hearing. At eight years there was no difference. What happened to the deaf children in one or two years to enable them to perform as well as the hearing on certain thinking tasks?

Surveying again the entire field of deaf-hearing differences or lack of differences, let us clarify what this means. When we assert that the deaf are deficient in language or that they are deficient on Piaget's tasks, we employ a similar sentence structure to express two different things. In the case of language, we simply say that the deaf, apart from a few individual exceptions, do not have the linguistic competence possessed by the hearing. There is no overlap in linguistic performance between the hearing and the deaf. The statement is true without reservations. Not so in the other case! When the investigator reports that the deaf make 4.20 errors and the hearing 5.87 errors on *Picture Sorting, Part 2,* and then proceeds to obtain a statistical significance for differences, such average results indicate in general a great amount of overlap. Thus many deaf children without linguistic competence perform better than many hearing children with linguistic competence, even though on the average, and significantly according to laws of probability, the linguistically competent hearing make fewer errors. Is it not obvious that such a state of affairs plays havoc with any serious theoretical linkage of linguistic competence and performance?

In general before attaching undue significance to observed differences, we should ask ourselves: How important are these differences when compared to intelligence in general and to the similarities observed in other experimental tasks? All this should be viewed against the constant factor of profound general linguistic deficiency versus easy, readily available linguistic competence.

In speaking to a group of teachers of the deaf, I touched upon the results which indicated that the deaf, who were equal on *Sameness* and *Symmetry,* were inferior to the hearing on *Opposites.* Should they teach the deaf the concept of opposite in a special way? I was asked, as if intellectual development consisted in accumulating singly learned verbal concepts? If the linguistically incompetent deaf never reached an operational level of thinking, or if they were consistently unable to comprehend mathematical or symbol-logic language, then we would have strong evidence for a decisive and general influence of language on thinking.

Compared to these possible effects, are not the observed effects trivial and superficial? Granted that the deaf are poorer in discovering the principle of opposition, what does this demonstrate regarding their intellectual structure?

If the deaf are slow in discovering an arbitrary principle in an experimental situation, what can one validly generalize from this performance? Rarely does such a situation occur in real life. Can one equate the gradual evolving of the known world with experimental discovery? Does a child "discover" the dimension of time in any way similar to his discovery that the experimenter rewards a certain form but disregards changing colors? In real life the clues for discovery are usually abundant and no effort is made to hide anything from the child. On the contrary, opportunities for learning are present in a fairly constant manner. The four-year-old child's comprehension or lack of comprehension of time concepts such as week, day, hour, minutes, has actually nothing to do with "discovery." If on such concepts, the deaf child showed some notable deficiency, that would perhaps be a serious indicator that absence of language adversely affects intellectual development.

Although deaf children are somewhat late in giving mature responses to Piaget's tasks, the principal point to keep in mind is that no deaf adult believes that the amount of liquid changes with changing containers or that there are more inhabitants of New Jersey than there are Americans. If the deaf appear rigid in a certain sense and adhere to a given viewpoint, is it because they have no understanding of the possible or that they have been socially trained to stay in the position they have found secure? If they fail to reason, is it because they cannot reason or because they are not motivated to reason?

As I observed deaf people, both in natural and experimental situations, I became increasingly convinced that the second alternative of each of the foregoing questions is more reasonable and scientifically justifiable. Deaf people behave as they do, not as a direct or necessary consequence of linguistic deficiency, but as a result of their social environment. This includes their early homes, their schooling, the deaf community within the hearing community, each with its social attitudes, stereotypes and other environmental factors. If the social environment could account for the observed intellectual behavior of the deaf, there would be no need to bring in the lack of linguistic competence, except insofar as it influences the social environment. In that case, we would look for a relation between social environment and intellectual development rather than between linguistic deficiency and intelligence, and we would inquire whether such a relation can be theoretically postulated and empirically established.

It is an incontestable fact that scientific thinking is to a great extent dependent on a favorable social environment. If our present society is characterized by a certain degree of sophistication, a willingness to examine facts and follow a reasonable argument, this does not imply that we are now more clever or have greater intellectual capacity than our forebears. In less developed cultures there is little opportunity for intellectual pursuits and consequently little motivation to engage in logical reasoning or scientific inquiry. The point stressed here relates to the social environment which does or does not motivate the inquiring mind. If we agree that a relation exists, we realize at once that linguistic accomplishment has nothing to do with the question. Any and all societies of hearing people employ a living language, and the fact that one culture encourages intellectual activity while another does not is unrelated to linguistic competence.

151

Bearing this in mind, it does not appear unreasonable to use a similar argument in the case of the intellectual behavior of the deaf. Could one, after independent observation of deaf children's early years, assert that they are experientially deprived? Could one furthermore infer from their scholastic setting that formal education does not provide much motivation for thinking and formal reasoning? If the picture of the deaf child and adolescent as sketched in Chapter II is in general true, deaf children are bound to be deficient in many ordinary experiences and occasions which motivate other children to ask questions, reason, and organize mentally. At the moment I readily admit that this experiential deficiency is directly related to linguistic deficiency, or more accurately, to the prevailing lack of ordinary communication. In Chapter XIV I shall return to this point, however, and argue against the inevitability of such consequences if our society and in particular our educators were willing to give up some preconceived assumptions about the necessary role of verbal language.

If we are justified in asserting that deaf children lack normal environmental stimulation toward an intellectual attitude, we can parsimoniously associate their observed intellectual retardation to this environmental handicap. It is striking that the intellectual area in which deaf people appear to fall behind the hearing has to do with discovery, with initiative on their part rather than with comprehension or application of concepts. In all these situations there seems to be an inability to look for reasons, not an inability to reason. It does not occur readily to the deaf to doubt or question perceptual appearances. We can call this an intellectual laziness or rigidity and the net result may at times appear to resemble intellectual incapacity.

We observed in a number of experimental situations that deaf children, once they grasped a principle, used and applied it as well as any hearing control subjects. In connection with the balancing of a scale, we found some deaf children woefully ignorant of how to coordinate weights and distances. With some slight hint on the part of the experimenter, these same deaf children were quite ready to grasp the principle and correctly apply it in new instances. The literature reports that some deaf children scored rather poorly on Raven's Progressive Matrices test. Our experience with the Raven test in individual testing in general did not support any notable deficiency on the part of the deaf. But occasionally we would come across a younger child who just could not succeed at all. At this point we gave some illustration of the correct procedure, by means of pointing and gestures. Frequently the child would catch on and repeat and continue far beyond that point at which he received help. It was because of these and similar happenings that we became convinced that a single approach from which to infer intellectual capacity was inadequate, certainly in the case of the deaf, and possibly for many persons who for different reasons fall outside the normal, middle-class urban society.

Thus far, it seems that the deficient performance of the deaf on some intellectual tasks can be more adequately accounted for by experiential than by linguistic deficiency, insofar as the former is more varied and flexible and relates specifically to the particular area in which the deaf are observed to fail, while linguistic deficiency is almost general and could only awkwardly be related to an intellectual performance that was not generally retarded. By experiential deficiency, we indicate socio-environmental factors which unfavorably influence the deaf child's development. This deficiency becomes manifest in the intellectual area, not so much in any lack of basic capacity to understand or to apply rational principles, but rather in a sphere which may be called intellectual-motivational and which concerns the spontaneous initiation or discovery of the inquiring mind.

I hasten to add that this experiential deficiency is of course related to the deaf child's incompetence in language. However, even without the addendum that such a relation is by no means inevitable, it behooves the investigator to differentiate a direct from an indirect influence and not to attribute to language what should properly be said of experience.

While the motivational aspect is rightly stressed, one should not forget the simple deficit in information which linguistic incompetence, again not inevitably, brings about and which may and frequently does affect performance on any task with familiar material. Verbal language is a convenient way of directing attention to different aspects of the environment or imparting information. For instance, pointing out a policeman in plain clothes stimulates a child's comprehension of the nonessential association between a profession and wearing apparel. Or we may tell a child that an eclipse of the moon will take place tonight, the first in so many years. It should be apparent that such information could be conveyed by pointing, gestures or pictures, but the fact is that parents of deaf children are not encouraged to communicate information by these means. Consequently, a deaf child is often seriously deficient in the knowledge of things familiar to hearing peers. This unfamiliarity with facts may then produce behavior which appears unintelligent to an observer but which follows logically from the behaving person's premises.

There are two ways in which the proposed hypothesis of a restrictive environment as main contributor to the deaf person's apparent intellectual deficiencies may be put to the test. The first would be to enrich the environment. If this were done, one would expect significant improvement in those areas where deaf people generally fail. (Suggestions for such an enrichment are made in Chapter XIV.) It is obvious that such a test would presuppose long-term training procedures and changes in educational policy which are not easy to accomplish.

The second test is more straightforward and, for our interest, even more enlightening. It would simply consist of obtaining a sample of persons who could be assumed to be culturally deprived, and comparing the performance of these persons with that of the deaf on some critical tasks. For such a sample, we turned to a school in a rural area with limited cultural advantages. The vast majority of pupils in this school came from homes where the father was a farm laborer or unskilled worker. We decided to test a comparable sample of these pupils on two representative tasks on which the deaf had shown retardation: Piaget's task of *Conservation of Amount of Liquid* and the task using *Logical Symbols*.

It will be recalled that on the first task the deaf were up to five years behind the hearing, although by the age of sixteen the deaf had reached the upper ceiling, i.e., they responded in a logical operational manner. On the *Symbol Discovery* task, the deaf failed at all age levels, even at the adult level, while the hearing generally succeeded at age twelve. The same deaf persons, however, performed similarly to hearing controls on the *Logical Symbol Use* task which required the application of these same logical symbols to various complicated instances. The *Symbol Use* task differentiated adults of high and low intelligence and showed the expected developmental curve.

In the case of the rural population, the result on judgment of *Amount of Liquid* is indicated on the lower part of Table 10 (p. 124) and graphically illustrated in Figure 8, below. From this evidence, the rural pupils fall midway between the deaf and the control hearing group. That is, it required an age level of about 13–14 years before general success was achieved, a level two years behind the control group and three years ahead of the deaf pupils. It should be noted that care was taken to equate the control and the rural groups on average intellectual ability.

The relevance of these findings to our thesis is twofold. There is confirmation of the theory that culture influences behavior on this kind of test and that, in general, developmental manifestation of logical thinking is a function not only

155

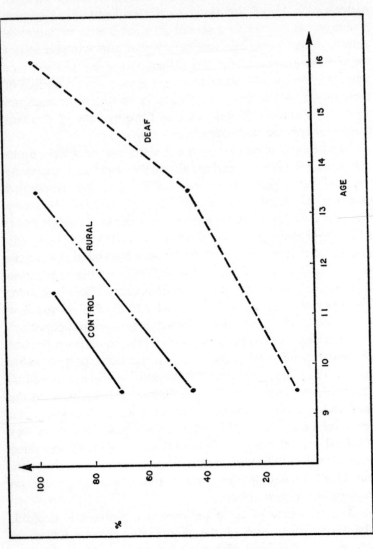

Figure 8. Percentage of subjects making correct judgments on conservation of amount of liquid at

156

of chronological age and intellectual capacity (IQ), but also of the social environment. Concerning the contribution of language to success on these tasks, the findings so far are somewhat inconclusive, although it is obvious that the rural children experienced no particular difficulty in comprehending the question of the examiner: "Which has more water?" and were quite competent in the English language. The deaf, on the other hand, had difficulty in understanding the question, even when it was asked in sign language.

It is suggested here that Piaget's task is bound up with a proper interpretation of the word "more." Thus the results can perhaps best be explained as a function of comprehending the word "more" and of comprehending the situational context in which the question occurred. The control group, enjoying the familiar use of language within a somewhat sophisticated urban society, had the best background for understanding and the deaf had the least. It seems quite reasonable to assume that the rare occasions on which the deaf child is exposed formally to a sophisticated question find him far less experienced than even the unsophisticated rural child who must have heard many similar questions, if not at home, then in school. The very fact that young deaf adults did comprehend the test situation, even though their linguistic skill had not appreciably improved, suggests strongly that language per se is not essential for success on this task. It is as if, at the age level where the ceiling is reached, the person can discover a question even before it is asked, i.e., he is sufficiently sophisticated to see the possibility of one or the other answer and finds it somewhat insulting to his intelligence to be questioned on this point. Possibly, for the deaf, this was not a fair test, since they had to reach an advanced level at which they could comprehend the meaning of the question by discovering it via the situation. The other groups were of course aided by their daily practice of linguistic communication.

In general, as has been pointed out by other writers, there

seems to be a fairly important discovery component in Piaget's tasks which may be responsible for the present difference in results. Factors which make for successful intellectual discovery cannot easily be specified, but culture and social environment are surely of great importance. Such reasoning may explain why no one has succeeded so far in employing Piaget's tasks as suitable tests for measuring IQ.

The performance of the rural sample on the two symbolic logic tasks proved to be an almost exact replica of the performance of the deaf. They failed, as badly as did the deaf, on the discovery aspect of the task (*Symbol Discovery*) and they succeeded as well as the deaf and also as well as the control groups on *Symbol Use*. (See last row of Table 13, p. 141, for the summarized results.) These rural subjects were certainly competent in their mother tongue, even though they may not have used this linguistic competence in a sophisticated manner. Under the aspect of linguistic competence, the rural sample was close to the control group and differed radically from the deaf. Yet their task performance was similar to that of the deaf with whom they had in common a lack of environmental stimulation. The rural pupils were apparently not interested in discovering a reason behind the associations they learned successfully in a rote-like manner. Thus, neither the deaf nor the rural sample spontaneously discovered or looked for reasons, even though these reasons stared them in the face—at least in the case of the twelve-year-old controls. On *Symbol Use,* however, when the situation was structured and only controlled reasoning could succeed, both groups showed their basic capacity for comprehension and application of logical rules.

These findings suggest the socio-environmental influence on discovery aspects of reasoning tasks as strongly as they do the lack of a decisive influence of linguistic competence on the capacity to comprehend and use logical symbols. The second point is central to the theme of the book, for it brings us back to the initial question on the relation of thinking and language. Just to state that results of the studies with linguistically incompetent deaf persons do at best indicate a limited, indirect influence, is not a satisfactory conclusion unless we are able to give a comprehensive view of intellectual growth and point out the place of language, whether it is close to or far from the center of its development. This attempt is made in Chapter XIII. Chapter XII provides some empirical evidence that bear on the question of verbal mediation.

Verbal Mediation and the Deaf

We now turn our attention to some of the studies in which deaf people performed remarkably like hearing controls. Oléron (1957) has already observed that in a number of symbolic tasks on which mediation was supposedly at work, the deaf were not inferior to the hearing. We have continued Oléron's line of experimentation by a systematic investigation of deaf children's behavior on some tasks in which leading psychologists theorize the presence of a mediating linguistic skill. If it were not for the existence of linguistically deficient persons, such as the deaf, I do not see how such theories could be tested directly. Hence it should be of concern to those psychologists who ascribe to language an almost necessary role in explaining success on certain behavioral tasks that deaf children succeed as well as hearing.

To repeat what was mentioned in a previous chapter, it has been postulated as a theoretical possibility that linguistic competence could account for the fact that children from about six years upward, after an initial discrimination task in which one dimension was reinforced and another had to be disregarded (e.g., blue correct, yellow incorrect, form irrelevant) would find it easier to reverse the color responses (e.g., yellow correct, blue incorrect) than to shift to a new dimension (e.g., circle correct, square incorrect) and disregard the previously relevant color dimension. With younger children and animals, frequently the opposite is true. They find it easier to shift to a new dimension than to reverse responses within a dimension. It is assumed that a covert linguistic response ("color") would control the outward response and thus facilitate shift within the dimension and make more difficult a shift to a new dimension.

Our research center has undertaken a variety of studies in which the "reversal" paradigm was employed. Youniss (1964) and Russell (1964) consistently found that linguistically incompetent deaf children performed similarly to the linguistically competent hearing children. In order to salvage the verbal theory, one may postulate that even deaf children around the age of six learn some single words like the names of colors and that the knowledge of these words enables the deaf children to behave as the hearing did. Against such a "cumulative" view of linguistic competence, there are a number of serious considerations of which two are made here. Deaf children at this age hardly ever know the vocabulary for the geometric forms which are commonly employed in these tasks, such as "circle" or "square." Secondly, many three- and four-year-old hearing children know the labels but apparently do not use them in performing reversal shift. Thus, these studies indicate rather strongly that the type of mediation postulated in the facilitation of reversal shift should not be exclusively identified with "verbal" mediation.

A similar conclusion follows from studies conducted by Youniss, in which deaf children were observed in conditions involving delay or spatial discontinuity. Delay and distance were chosen as constituting conditions which "verbal mediators" may conceivably help to "bridge." Again, illiterate deaf children showed a performance level similar to hearing children of comparable age. In yet another study, Furth and Youniss (1964) although not working within a strict reversal paradigm, discovered that the deaf had less, rather than more, difficulty compared to the hearing in associating reversed colors. The following study is reported in somewhat greater detail because some interesting differences between deaf and hearing children were observed and because it deals with a learning task which is considered by many psychologists as a crucial indicator of symbolic functioning.

Experiment 12: Double Alternation in Hearing and Deaf Children (Pufall, 1965)

This study addressed itself to double alternation behavior, its acquisition and transfer in deaf and hearing children. The principle of alternation implies a regular change in response behavior. A procedure in which a person, faced with the choice of one of two responses, would, in order to be correct, have to change regularly from one response on one trial to the other on the next trial, back to the first response again on the third trial, and so on, would exemplify simple alternation. Double alternation means a change of response every third trial, e.g., right, right, left, left, right, right, left, etc.

Past research suggested that acquisition of the principle of double alternation (DA) is a difficult achievement for animals and younger children. Investigators hypothesized that symbolic and particularly verbal capacity may provide the means for success on DA, the extent of which can best be tested by transfer tasks. Oléron, in an experiment with a small number of deaf and hearing children, considered his results supported the notion that verbal ability was crucial for success on DA. The present study employed larger numbers of deaf and hearing subjects over a wider age range and across a greater variety of transfer tasks, with a view toward clarifying the role of language on DA behavior.

SUBJECTS AND PROCEDURE

Twelve hearing and twelve deaf children were selected at each of five age levels from 4 to 9 with age 8 eliminated. The deaf children were uniformly deaf at birth, or before age three, and they and the hearing children were judged by teachers to be of average learning ability. For the acquisition task, the child faced a wooden board which had two doors on it. The child was required to look for a reward behind one of the two doors. The experimenter placed the reward (a checker) in double alternation fashion, twice behind one door and twice behind the other door. A maximum of 60 trials was given and the criterion for success was 10 consecutive correct choices by the child. Task II, the first transfer task, substituted two blocks for the doors, and a light, controlled by the experimenter, was used to indicate the correct choice. Number of trials and criterion were the same as on acquisition. The first two tasks had position (left, right) as relevant and no obviously irrelevant response aspects.

The next three tasks introduced by way of interference some changing dimensions which the subject had to disregard. For Task III, blocks were used, but these blocks had two different colors and the child had to continue with double alternation from left to right while disregarding the color. Task IV employed two wooden forms of the same color, a triangle and a circle, and the child had to choose the triangle twice, the circle twice and so forth, disregarding the position of the forms. Finally, on Task V, the same blocks as on Task III were used, but this time the relevant variable was color and position had to be disregarded. The reinforced choices for the child were one color twice, the other color twice, and so forth. Only those children who succeeded on I continued on

163

II, and only those who succeeded on II were given Tasks III to V. These latter tasks uniformly had 20 trials and a criterion of seven consecutive correct choices.

RESULTS AND DISCUSSION

The results of this study are summarized in Table 14 in terms of the number of children who were successful on each task. The entries on the table for the first task are based on 12 children, while the number of children who performed on Tasks II to V varied according to success on Tasks I or II. The last column presents a total score of number of successes for each age group.

In the case of the hearing group, one observes a rapid increase in number of successes between ages 4 and 6. At age 5 acquisition reaches a ceiling with transfer performance falling off and reaching its apparent ceiling only the following year. This discrepancy between acquisition and transfer illustrates that the generality of the DA principle was still labile at age 5 and became serviceable only at age 6.

Table 14—Number of Successful Hearing (H) and Deaf (D) Subjects on a Series of Double Alternation Tasks

	ACQUI-SITION		II		III		IV		V		ALL TASKS	
Age	H	D	H	D	H	D	H	D	H	D	H	D
4	5	2	2	2	0	0	0	0	0	1	7	5
5	8	2	4	0	1	0	1	0	2	0	16	2
6	8	10	8	6	1	1	4	1	4	0	25	18
7	9	9	9	9	1	2	5	2	7	9	31	30
9	8	10	7	9	3	4	4	5	5	6	27	29

As to a comparison between the deaf and the hearing, it is at once obvious that no reliable difference emerged at age 4 and also at ages 7 and above. The most striking difference occurred at age 5 in the small proportion of deaf children who were successful on acquisition, while at age 6 the slight retardation of the deaf is due, not to failure on acquisition, but rather to their falling off on transfer tasks. In summary, then, at ages 5 and 6, the deaf trailed behind the hearing about one year with no difference before and after these ages.

Such results would constitute evidence for the necessity of linguistic skill for successful DA performance if one could reasonably assume that these deaf children, through formal language training and by mastery of a vocabulary of perhaps 20 to 60 words, have been turned into verbal persons by the age of 7. We have, however, sound evidence to reject such an assumption, insofar as the deaf children of this study were without exception incompetent in comprehending connected language.

Perhaps the main point of interest for the verbal mediation hypothesis is the fact that at and after age 7, the linguistically incompetent deaf child acquires and transfers the DA principle as readily as do hearing controls. It seems that the slight retardation observed in this experiment can well be accounted for by the general experiential deficiency with which deaf children grow up.

Twin Study

A second investigation we wish to consider in some detail has some bearing on verbal mediation as it is conceived by a number of developmental psychologists who ascribe to verbal language a uniquely important role in intellectual growth. Some years ago, I had the opportunity of participating in a psychological investigation of deaf twins as part of a larger project, a fuller description of which is found in Rainer et al. (1964, particularly Chapter 4). Here I would like to describe two four-year-old girls who were monozygotic, hence identical twins of deaf parents, yet one twin was deaf, the other hearing.

In general, their social and informal behavior was strik-

165

ingly alike. They communicated within their family by means of gestures and manual signs. It was not surprising that in such an environment the expressive verbal behavior of the hearing co-twin was seriously retarded although she comprehended simple language suitable to her age and at times interpreted remarks to her deaf co-twin. According to the Vineland Social Maturity Scale, both twins scored exactly alike and rated about one year in advance of their age. These girls were tested on the Merrill-Palmer Scale, excluding verbal subtests, and almost identical performance was observed. The deaf girl obtained a mental age of two months above her chronological age, the hearing girl a mental age of one month above.

Two conclusions may be drawn from these data. As regards the deaf child, she was in the fortunate position of being truly accepted by her deaf parents and she experienced the benefit of early, easy communication by manual signs which included some spelling. In this four-year-old deaf child there was no objective indication of any abnormal development either intellectually, socially, or emotionally. This indicates that no untoward effects follow automatically from early deafness or lack of verbal language. Regarding the hearing co-twin, the general similarity of her behavior in natural and experimental situations with the deaf twin's behavior was quite pronounced, as if competence in verbal language made no appreciable difference. We wondered at the time whether this similarity would persist and some possible changes in favor of the language-competent girl were predicted.

Rainer et al. report that these twins were in fact re-tested three years later. Again, their scores on two different performance tests of general intelligence were within the range of individual chance variability. While the deaf twin was now attending a school for the deaf, the co-twin attended an ordinary school and functioned as a normally hearing child although some audiometric hearing loss was noticed. It is notable from the summarizing tables of this report that there were five identical twin-pairs in which one twin was deaf and could not acquire language in a normal fashion while the other co-twin was hearing or hard-of-hearing. Our twin girls were the only pair who tested alike on the Arthur Point Scale. In the case of the other four pairs, the deaf twin showed some retardation relative to the best-hearing co-twin.

It would seem germane to contrast these twins with those who were observed by Luria and Yudovich (1959). Both twins studied by the Soviet investigators and discussed before in Chapter V on p. 64 were hearing, but socially, mentally, intellectually, and linguistically immature. With separation from each other and some special attention, their behavior improved remarkably in all these aspects. The twins described above were similar in age to the Soviet twins, but they were socially and emotionally developed, one was deaf and the other hearing or hard-of-hearing. The former was without verbal language and the latter had verbal language, yet both behaved normally and tested quite similarly on performance scales of intelligence. A high degree of similarity is a usual phenomenon in the case of identical twins. Yet in the present sample one co-twin had obtained linguistic competence and the other used gestures and manual signs for communication.

While the Soviet study is commonly interpreted as showing the controlling impact of verbal skill on early behavior, a comparison with the present twin study would make an explanation in terms of normal socialization, i.e., a normal living contact with the environment, more compelling. Either mastery or lack of verbal language did not seem to make much difference in the twins described here, but lack of adequate social contact, whether for deaf or hearing children, is known from other sources to retard development, including intellectual maturation.

It is quite true that the deaf girl of the twin study did communicate freely with her parents and siblings and consequently was not lacking some kind of language. She merely lacked verbal language. Yet scholars, such as Werner or Luria, do ascribe to verbal language some unique quality which differentiates it from other kinds of communication. Particularly, they emphasize that language lends itself readily to the mediation of overt behavior, first as covert or inner language, and then as "that in which or by which" we think and reason in a mature manner.

It has been shown that the intelligence of linguistically deprived deaf persons in development and maturity seems not basically different from that of the hearing. Only in a few special cases, like *Opposition* or *Classification Shift* and of course on all "verbal" tasks, do linguistic habits directly influence test performance. In other situations it does not seem altogether reasonable to link differences in performance level directly with difference in linguistic competence.

In a number of areas in which verbal mediation or control has been proposed as crucial, deaf children were observed to do as well as the hearing. While the deaf were often slow in discovering a principle of reasoning—a motivational-intellectual characteristic which can be associated with their intellectually restrictive environment—the deaf adults seem to have the ability of hearing persons to comprehend and logically apply principles and concepts.

Such are the conclusions based upon experimental evidence with regard to the deaf. The implications of these findings bring us back to the more basic and general question about the process of human thinking. If we must accept the fact that the deaf think, even though they do not have verbal language, how do they do it? How can we explain the growth and mature manifestation of human thinking without language? Is there such a thing as thinking without language?

Jean Piaget is among the contemporary psychologists to whom we can turn for a possible explanation. For many others verbal language is theoretically so closely linked to intelligence that they would be forced by the logic of their theories to give a clear "no" to the last question.

At this point in our inquiry, we are actually no longer asking whether it is possible to think logically without enjoying linguistic competence. We know that it is possible with a degree of certitude that we would not dare assert if empirical observation of deaf persons had not provided a natural *experimentum crucis*. It remains to dissolve the dilemma created by this knowledge, which appears contrary to many popular, unanalyzed assumptions about the role of language. Unless we can explain the growth of intelligence without basing it on language, we will prefer, like Galileo's contemporaries, to close our eyes or look in another direction.

CHAPTER XIII

Development of Thinking and Language

Scientific progress is dependent on painstaking observation and analysis of facts but it also depends on the theoretical positions and frequently unanalyzed assumptions which prompted the explorations in the first place. These assumptions are of particular concern to psychological science in its attempt to cut a path of understanding within the thicket of human living. It is difficult enough to push beyond the frontiers of the known into unmapped regions of knowledge, and it is apparently more arduous to look upon events which are supposed to be familiar to everybody in a new light. Such was the task which empirical psychology faced in its beginning and although the climate has changed considerably in the past hundred years, this task is still very much with us.

The survey presented in Chapters IV and V should impress the reader with the overriding importance of the theoretical viewpoints taken by investigators who study thinking. Assume thinking to be a supra-material activity and you relegate it to the province of philosophers and theologians. Assume that the way to study an event is to analyze it into units and elements, and you will attempt to do this in the investigation of thinking. Postulate the need to reduce all behavior to neural events, and you will explore and theorize regarding the millions of cells and structures of the nervous system.

There is no one criterion by which we can judge one or the other theoretical position to be correct, since these positions are essentially viewpoints which in themselves cannot be right or wrong. The fruitfulness of a theory lies in its scientific fecundity, in the broad scope of its unifying principles and in the formal and specific power of explaining and predicting by means of a minimum of *ad hoc* principles.

Scientific fecundity requires that a scientific theory serve empirical science by leading to hypotheses which are testable through observation. The breadth of a theory refers to a degree of generality in which phenomena related organically on an objective plane are encompassed on the theoretical plane in a systematic unity. Finally and most importantly, principles which relate specifically to the phenomenon to be investigated should flow from the theory. These principles should bear on critical or inherently basic aspects of the phenomenon. There should be no need to multiply principles to explain one basic fact which may appear under differing contextual conditions. As an illustration, a theory which links pulse rate with thinking, even though significant covariations may perhaps be observed, would be of no value to a scientific investigator unless he could point to a specific and inherent relation between the two phenomena. Likewise, the observation that scores on a vocabulary test correlate substantially with general intelligence level, is of minimal help for a scientific appraisal of intelligence unless a direct, formal link is demonstrated between intellectual processes and familiarity with words.

For historical reasons which have been touched upon repeatedly, the modern American psychologist is supposed to avoid "mental" terms, as "to know, to will, the mind," under pain of being called unscientific. While such an attitude was perhaps in the past an understandable reaction against the indiscriminate use of these terms, today, with a somewhat maturer attitude, psychologists should certainly not shy away from words which describe essential parts of our common experience. Rather, we should make an effort to explain them in terms which make them amenable to a behavioral scientific approach.

In its broadest sense, thinking like any other behavior implies an interaction between organism and environment, or, in biological terms, an adaptation of the living organism to his environment. Thinking, moreover, carries a subjective connotation, with the emphasis on an internal activity or some habitual capacity as distinct from objective functioning or acting which can be described as a single, observable event. Thinking has a meaning close to the word knowing with the difference that thinking emphasizes an ongoing process, while knowledge emphasizes a habitual state. Our language permits the use of the phrase "to know" with reference to human and subhuman organisms, e.g.: "This child knows that $3 + 4 = 7$" or "A robin knows when the winter is approaching and prepares accordingly." But in a sentence like "A plant knows where to look for water" the use of the word "knows" is recognized as metaphorical.

In behavioral and linguistic terms, there is little difference in describing the three events: the plant moves its roots in the direction of getting an optimum water supply when water is scarce; the bird prepares his flight south at the approach of cold weather; and the child responds with "seven" when asked for the sum of three and four. A mere external description of events does not allow us to differentiate kinds of knowledge and to ascribe knowledge to the latter two events but not to the first.

At this point we can decide that thinking and knowing are

equally useless terms for human behavior and for plant functioning, particularly if for other reasons we are strongly inclined to assume that behavioral principles which are valid for animals can encompass the gamut of human behavior. As far as animals are concerned, it is quite true that the term "to know" is not an indispensable word in the description of animal behavior. But to omit a description of thinking and knowing from the behavioral repertoire of humans, requires a *tour de force* which we are not prepared to make, all the more so since we are not bound to the assumption that thinking in man should be explainable in terms applicable to knowing in subhumans. Here we expand what was briefly touched on in Chapter III.

"Man, as [positivist] science is able to reconstruct him today, is an animal like the others" says the anthropologist Teilhard de Chardin (1959) who attempts to place the phenomenon of the human mind within the entire evolutionary development of the universe. He points out that anatomically, the differences between man and anthropoids are so minimal that zoologists are justified in classifying both in the same super-family, the hominidae. Teilhard continues, "Yet, to judge by the biological results of his advent, is he not in reality something altogether different? Morphologically the leap was extremely slight, yet it was the concomitant of an incredible commotion among the spheres of life—there lies the whole human paradox" (p. 163).

Teilhard argues further that "science, in its present-day reconstruction of the world, neglects an essential factor, or rather, an entire dimension of the universe." This neglected factor is the topic of our consideration: human thinking or, reflective thinking, as Teilhard calls it. He states that humans do not only recognize, but they recognize themselves; they do not only know, but they know that they know. Teilhard does not appeal to philosophical arguments, he points to empirical evidence: "If the animal could know reflectively it would long ago have multiplied its inventions and developed a system of internal constructions that could not have escaped our observation" (p. 165).

By what signs can the scientist observe these internal constructions? Knowledge in itself, like thinking, cannot be observed, since it is by definition an internal, subjective act or state. Is there any criterion which is inherently linked to thinking and at the same time objectively observable? Some knowledge is associated with objective symbols, that is, with signs which are produced or producible by the knowing person and which relate indirectly to the thing signified via the knowing person. Another type of knowledge is linked with cues or stimuli which are externally given and which directly relate to the thing signified. This second type of sign is called a signal. Behavior associated with signals, in distinction from behavior associated with symbols, does not seem to require the intermediate link of a knowing organism.

The presence of a signal, e.g., the shape of a moving object, is only observed in direct connection with a response which it determines, e.g., fear reactions on the part of certain animals. The presence of a symbol, on the other hand, such as a drawing or a written message, can be recognized without external specific action. A symbol by itself demonstrates or manifests that there is a state of knowing within a living organism. Whatever objective events a symbol signifies, it does so only through the intermediary of a knowing person. Symbols abound in human life. If one wishes to investigate the symbol and the symbolic activities of men at large, one is bound to recognize the special mode of knowing which characterizes human symbolic behavior.

The foundation of any living experience, the most basic psychological act in the process of adaptation or learning is what James calls the sense of "identity" or sameness. To learn through experience, even in the most primitive mode of living, means to react in a similar manner to similar kinds of stimulation, to react to some event not as completely new, but as familiar in some respects. The identity response is at the base of instinctual action patterns, of stimulus substitution in conditioned learning, and of all types of behavioral generalizations. It also lies at the root of any knowledge.

James (1950, Vol. 1, pp. 459 ff) refers to this *sense of sameness* as "the very keel and backbone of our thinking." And he adds that this sense of sameness concerns the point of view of the mind's structure alone. "We are psychologizing, not philosophizing. That is, we do not care whether there be any *real* sameness in *things* or not, or whether the mind be true or false in its assumption of it. . . . Without the psychological sense of identity, sameness might rain down upon us from the outer world and we be none the wiser."

It is intriguing to consider that Piaget's most fundamental attributes of intellectual structure relate closely to this notion of sameness. For Piaget, the very first manifestation of the budding intelligence is object "constancy," the ability to react to things-as-known-out-there, as stable and same; the beginnings of logical operations are observed in judgments of "conservation" concerning the identity of a certain aspect of the object against perceptual changes in other aspects; and the hallmark of mature logical thinking is "reversibility," the ability hypothetically to consider any state along a continuum of possibilities as potentially equal to any other state and to return to the same state from which a proposed operation took its beginning.

I am tempted to compare Piaget's insight in the matter of intelligence to the revolutionary viewpoint of Freud regarding human motivation. Freud once and for all abolished the cherished dream of a humanity being guided in the main by reason with a capital R; he demonstrated that most of human motivation is rather a caricature of reason or rationalization in the wider sense. He bridged the extremes of reason and un-

175

reason by making abnormality more normal and normality more abnormal. Piaget also abolished the idealistic dream of a ready-made intelligence and bridged the extremes by pointing to the functional similarity of knowing in all its stages and to the specific structural changes which characterize thinking in the developing person. At the same time his theory removed the need to fear an unscientific discontinuity in differentiating types of thinking. He discovered the beginning of characteristically human or intelligent thinking in early developmental stages, typical of infants and subhuman animals. Piaget looked for the basis of intelligent thinking not in concepts which are abstracted from object-made images, ready-made by some mysterious mind or through the linguistic society, but in the almost imperceptible "knowing" reaction of a one-year old infant towards objects.

Piaget believes that careful observation of the search behavior of infants allows him to infer at a certain age the transition from one type of behavior to another. Earlier behavior can be accounted for by sensory-motor reactions to environmental events, but the new way of behaving occuring at the transition period indicates that the objective stimulus event is transformed into a known event. The behavior is then no longer a reaction to objective stimuli but is beginning to be controlled by stimuli-as-known or knowing. What does knowing involve at the threshold of intelligence? It is related to the very basis of all knowledge, namely the sense of identity. The child has reached a stage in which objects persist even though they are no longer present to the senses. In other words, objects take on a permanence and are regarded as the same even when not present to the senses. Such an achievement, modest as it is, far from being natively or objectively given, is the work of the thinking child, the first fruit of knowing on which any further knowing is based. Piaget calls this turning point "the formation of objects" or "object constancy."

Before his turning point an infant will be keenly attracted

to a glittering toy, yet the moment it is removed from sight, the infant's behavior seems to indicate that the toy has simultaneously disappeared from his mind. Not so afterwards. The child's active search for the hidden object suggests that the toy has now become a vital part of his behavior, that there is an internal representation of the toy which controls the child's behavior, so that with regard to the child we can use the phrase, "he knows that there is a toy"; while before we would simply assert that he reacts to the toy. Werner and Kaplan (1963, pp. 9 ff, pp. 67 ff) stress this distinction between "action on things" from "contemplation of things" and add that a prerequisite for symbolic activity is a developmental stage which regards things as stable and "out there" rather than as things to which an organism merely reacts to satisfy a certain biological need.

Even at this level we can point to some characteristics of thinking which will remain typical for this activity in all its further manifestations. First, object constancy refers to an all-inclusive state and not to a single event. Thinking is always to be regarded as a generalized mode of behavior and can in no way be conceived as a simple cumulation of single elements or connections. Hence it would make as little sense to assert that an infant has formed the object of "bottle" in isolation, but not objects of equally familiar things, as to say that a solitary mature concept can become manifest in somebody's behavior. This conclusion leads to the second observation that thinking is always related to an internal organized structure. The best way to describe thinking is precisely to infer the characteristics of this internal structure. Thus one may assume that permanence of objects "out there" would correspondingly lead to a permanence of a self which is differentiated from other objects. The structure of object permanence requires as a corresponding counterpart the formation of a stable self.

A third and last consideration refers to thinking as an activity, an internal action which corresponds to the sensory-

177

motor schema of the previous period and is habitually associated with or accompanied by observable organismic events. It is conceivable that a child in recognizing a toy makes a certain grasping movement which prepares him to react appropriately to the object. With the advent of object constancy, such grasping movements may still be present and may even be an inherent part of the child's thinking—it would be unnatural for a two year old child to comprehend the word "hand" without visibly moving his own hands. Consequently it seems reasonable to regard sensory-motor schemas and thinking processes as functionally alike insofar as they are both actions—one is externally observable, the other only inferable.

Once the child has reached the stage of a stable universe which includes his self as a stable part, the child's development of thinking evolves most conspicuously in his symbolic or representational activity. Piaget subsumes under the symbolic function a wide range of children's activities, including imitation, imagination, play, dreams, and language. The symbolic function is that specific aspect of the thinking person which results in the formation of symbols. Under the term symbol we have to understand an objective or external event, at least from the standpoint of the person experiencing it. This symbolic event refers directly to the thinking person and indirectly to the objective event signified by the symbol.

If Piaget stresses that the stable perception of a present object is the result of an internal thinking activity, it is not surprising that he says the same thing and even more strongly about the image which the mind experiences. He dismisses the common temptation to regard a visual image in terms of a passively received picture, rather he links it to active, deferred imitation. Children perceive the functioning of an object within their known world and consequently are prone to imitate some functional aspect in the absence of the original. They will imitate the mother's sweeping the floor, the movement of the cars or the popular songs to which they are exposed. Such activity is not a parrot-like copying but the embodiment of an internal transformation with which the child reacts to these events. Under this aspect, deferred imitation is an observable symbolic activity which, as it were, enlarges the scope of the known object by extending its identity or permanence in time and space. Imitation is thus the first true symbol; it is produced by a knowing person, it is objectively present and by itself it represents an object-as-known.

According to Piaget, an image, whether it is kinesthetic, visual or in some other modality, is a diminutive imitation, the issue of an activity similar to the one resulting in outward imitation, but limited to an internal experiencing. It has a function similar to imitation but is freer and becomes more readily available since it is not tied to gross muscle movements. Its presence cannot directly be observed in another person, rather is it inferred from the child's developing spatial orientation, drawing, memory performance, and other kinds of behavior which are reasonably assumed to be under the active control of an internal state of knowing. An image also, as far as it is experienced by the knowing person or reflectively described, is a symbol, representing its object via the knowing person.

The experiencing of dreams is clearly related to imagery. The symbolic significance of a dream could only come as a surprising discovery to Freud's contemporaries who were imbued with the then prevailing "rational" view of human intelligence. This view considered images to be photo-like copies of sensory impressions, to be looked at by rational consciousness. In Piaget's opinion, thinking is an activity that is by itself outside of awareness. The internal events that one may at times become conscious of, are not the processes of thinking but the products of thinking, that is, symbols. These symbols may be in the form of images or words.

Playing, the typical childhood activity, can be seen as the use of an alien object in the service of a known object. Children will get hold of a pencil and two ashtrays and use the pencil as a car and the ashtrays as blocks of houses. Playing is thus a symbolic activity or a symbol which finds its meaning in the thinking child. To understand play, one has to see it as a product of symbolic thinking.

The spontaneous need and joy which children manifest in their playing is but another instance of countless other activities at all age levels which would be utterly incomprehensible if, following Susanne Langer, one did not postulate a need to know and to symbolize as a universal characteristic of man's behavior.

If our basic needs were really just those of lower creatures much refined, we should have evolved a more realistic language than in fact we have. If the mind were essentially a recorder and transmitter, typified by the simile of the telephone-exchange, we should act very differently from the way we actually do. Certainly no learning-process has caused man to believe in magic; yet word-magic is a common practice among primitive peoples and so is vicarious treatment—burning in effigy, etc.—where the proxy is plainly a mere symbol of the desired victim. Another strange, universal phenomenon is ritual. It is obviously symbolic, except where it is aimed at concrete results, and then it may be regarded as a communal form of magic. Now, all magical and ritual practices are hopelessly inappropriate to the preservation and increase of life. My cat would turn up his nose and his tail at them. To regard them as mistaken attempts to control nature, as a result of wrong synapses, or crossed wires in the brain, seems to me to leave the most rational of animals too deep in the slough of error. If a savage in his ignorance of physics tries to make a mountain open its caverns by dancing round it, we must admit with shame that no rat in a psychologist's maze would try such patently ineffectual methods of opening a door. Nor should such experiments be carried on, in the face of failure, for thousands of years; even morons should learn more quickly than that (Langer, 1964, pp. 41–42).

Amid this variety of symbolic activity which extends over the total range of behavior, including its social and emotional parts—aspects which are here omitted for the sake of space and clarity—there also takes place the acquisition and use of language. Language too is a symbol and as a symbol-system it is acquired by the growing child in living contact with his linguistic environment, much the same way as he learns the concepts of space, time or causality through an exposure to the physical environment. The linguistic symbol is unique in that it provides a ready-made systematic symbolic representation of society's experience which can serve as a universal means of social communication. Like any other symbol, its learning and use is the product or manifestation of the knowing child and for its meaning, or the thing signified, we have to look, not in our dictionary, but to the thinking structure of the speaking child.

As Piaget describes the structure of the growing child's intelligence from about age 1.5 to 5, he uses the symbolic activity, including language, as a way of making inferences from behavior to inner structure. He stresses the gradual grasp of such basic notions as time, causality, spatial orientation, grouping of objects. They are attained at a level short of true concepts inasmuch as mental processes are still too closely associated with the perceptually or imaginatively given object. The child's thinking during this period is characterized by the total involvement of the child in his present state. The typical pre-school child lives wholly in the present. He does not clearly differentiate one experience from the next or relate one to another. He does not ask for reasons and accepts the immediately given reality at face value. Piaget has coined the term "ego-centric" for this attitude of uncritical self-involvement. It should be clear that this attitude has nothing to do with the common meaning of the word as a synonym of selfishness.

Four or five years after the first indications of representative thinking, around the age of six, the child manifests the beginning of logical operations and logical concepts.

181

With the appearance of operational intelligence, thinking activity has, as it were, made a full turn. At the younger, sensory-motor level it was steeped in and almost undifferentiated from practical activity; at the operational level, even though retaining the characteristics of a human activity, it is no longer formally tied to external activity. This transformation of thinking is not something that takes place during a certain limited period of time, like physiological changes at puberty. There is a constant almost imperceptible growth from the first sensory-motor reflexes to behavior that demonstrates the mature comprehension of logical concepts.

If Piaget had not succeeded in presenting the intellectual growth in organically related stages, if he had not encompassed perceptual and symbolic activity within the same intellectual organization, if he had accepted our common way of speaking of the perception of external objects and the self as natively given, if finally he had looked for different *ad hoc* explanations and extra-psychological variables, his view would not be so convincing. Both Freud and Piaget were able to make decisive contributions in psychology because they analyzed and delved into psychological problems heretofore relegated to philosophy, but they looked into the real life of the developing person for answers to their questions. They did not philosophize on the essence of the soul or the nature of the intellect; but they did what James called "psychologize," that is, their theories were under the control of behavioral observation. Neither Freud nor Piaget was inclined to delimit their view of life by extra-psychological considerations whether they were logical, mathematical, mechanical, or physiological. Consequently they describe vital aspects of human life and the behavioral scientist can find in their theories a fruitful approach to the study of human motivation or thinking.

When it is asserted that operational intelligence is not formally tied to sensory-motor activity, the word "formal" should be understood from the viewpoint of a psychological theory. In this case it means that intelligent activity at the mature stage of operational functioning is no longer specifically and inherently associated with sensory-motor activity of any kind. Before this stage, during the many years of slow transformation, there was an essential aspect of thinking which was tied to organismic activity in the form of the symbolic function. Genetically speaking, operational intelligence is internalized sensory-motor activity in the same sense in which Freud states that present artistic creating is a transformation or sublimation of primitive sexual and aggressive instincts. Piaget's internalization and Freud's sublimation denote a developmental-genetic aspect of functional similarity between two phenomena which are quite specific and quite different.

Both scientists were at pains to show and accent the continuity of developing life. For Freud, man's most sublime strivings were mature manifestations of forces which are at work at the more primitive and organic level of early bodily affection. Freud thought some of the attributes and functional characteristics of these dynamic forces could be discovered in a clearer fashion at earlier developmental levels. Similarly, Piaget inferred some constant and essential conditions of thinking from the behavior of infants. If other scientists interested in thinking were looking at the child's behavior at all, this was mainly to note points in which children's thinking differed from adults', not points of similarity.

Consequently, in spite of developmental continuity, the present does not find its "formal" explanation in the past. Freud did not wish to give the impression that a certain infantile history was a condition *sine qua non* for creativity. Most people with a similar background do not become creators and most creators have different past histories. In a similar manner, operational intelligence, although it is rooted in a past of sensory-motor activity, is no longer tied to or specifically explainable in terms of any particular organismic activity, even though it may well be accompanied by it.

During an earlier period, thinking was still tied to the kind of organismic activity in which the symbolic activity consists. Piaget refers here to representational thinking or schemas. But the operational period of thinking differs from the preceding period precisely in that we no longer think "in" any internally perceptible activity. If we do become conscious of images or movements, these are merely organismic accompaniments and not an inherent part of thinking.

Characteristically, in studying the growing intelligence of the young child, Piaget looks to symbolic activity in the form of play, imitation, and imagery. He discusses the child's verbal judgments to the extent that they reveal his thinking. A child's view of the world is intimately related to his symbolic activity. For Piaget, symbolic thinking is halfway between the two extremes of no representational thinking in the sensory-motor period of action—or practical intelligence—and the formal thinking of operational intelligence. Strictly speaking, the period of transition which is called pre-operational belongs still to sensory-motor intelligence insofar as the formal break between thinking and sensory-motor activity only takes place at the operational level. The symbolic function can be viewed as an organic outgrowth of sensory-motor intelligence. It would be futile to ask whether the symbolic activity determines the growth of intelligence or vice versa. The point we wish to stress is that at a pre-operational level it makes sense to assert that the child thinks "in symbols," i.e., internalized, ego-involved sensory-motor schemas. But at the operational level, a similar wording "to think in" is formally a contradiction, because operational thinking implies a break with any specific tie to sensory-motor activity. In other words, operational differs from pre-operational thinking exactly in that the latter constitutes a "thinking in," while the former does not.

If this view of intellectual development is correct, it would follow that symbolic activity, in Piaget's sense, is no longer characteristic for adults, but of course common observation tells us that nothing is further from the truth. Here again I can see a parallel between Freud and Piaget. Freud is often blamed for presenting a one-sided view of human personality and Piaget too may give the impression he is postulating a unique paradigm for thinking, one modeled after logic. Such blame is unjustified. Neither of the two wrote a textbook in general psychology. Each was concerned with some specific aspects of human behavior and stressed them accordingly. Piaget's concern was the growth of logical thinking and his observations and theoretical views are geared accordingly. Moreover, I have failed to point out that Piaget employs the term "symbolic" more in a Freudian than symbolic-logic sense. For Piaget symbolic implies always some degree of ego-centrism, some lack of objective comprehension which is the mark of mature logical thinking. In fact, to the extent that language can be the means of expressing logical thinking, Piaget differentiates language from other symbols and gives it the name of "conventional sign" as distinguished from a "motivated sign" or "symbol" in the narrow sense.

However, there is more to it than this. Piaget's interest, being centered on logical thinking, was obliged to turn to symbolic activity during the child's pre-operational stage since in this activity the growing intelligence becomes manifest. But from four or five years onward Piaget worked almost exclusively with logical thinking of some kind or other and has been more interested in demonstrating what children at the pre-operational period could not do than what they could do. As he concentrated on these children's illogical, or better, prelogical judgments of quantity, number or class, a perusal of his writings may give the impression that thinking from seven years upward was on all occasions operational, discursive, logical.

The fact is, of course, that logical thinking, even in adults, is a relatively rare event and that the overwhelming majority of thinking is steeped in sensory-motor or symbolic, ego-motivated activity. The observation that language can be used in expressing logical activity and that we are frequently engaged in linguistic behavior of some sort or other should not tempt us to believe that most of this activity is controlled by operational thinking.

Finally, as Langer has indicated so decisively, discursive logical thinking is merely one end-product of the growing human intelligence. The larger part of thinking never reaches the discursive stage and remains symbolic in Piaget's and Freud's sense. That particular aspect of human intellective activity is not gone into at any great length by Piaget. It suffices to mention that there are vast areas of mature human activity which are not logical in the sense that they could be expressed in logical language, yet they are definitely the expression of mature thinking or intelligence. Such activity includes works of art in their manifold varieties, music, poetry, fine art, dancing, etc. Ritual, religious, contemplative, and moral actions are other activities that are not exhausted by logical reasoning.

In fact, thinking permeates all human activity, whether it is social, emotional, or moral. One can recognize a development and a maturity in all these areas corresponding to the actual state of intellectual growth. One is justified in calling these activities symbolic insofar as these "preter-logical" activities represent internal intellectual control. Moreover the meaning of the activities has to be found in the thinking state to which they refer.

Some symbolic activity or event may be fully conscious and recognized, as in some social manners or it may be hidden to the person behaving and only gradually and by dint of special methods revealed to the trained eye of a psychoanalyst. The salute to the flag, the enjoyment of music, the gathering around the table for a meal, the title after a name, an endless variety of outward kinds of behavior, events and objects, all have their symbolic character by the fact that they issue from a thinking person and refer back to him. Play, dreams, imitation, and images belong in a similar category of symbols and as they occur at an earlier stage of development, they were singled out by Piaget to illustrate the growth of childhood intelligence during the "symbolic" period from 1.5 to about 6 to 8 years of age.

Depending on the function which intelligence serves, one may consider symbolic events along a continuum from outer to inner directed. The bizarre mannerism of a schizophrenic is symbolic and refers to his highly private individual experiences while the letter π as a mathematical symbol, is a public conventional symbol which refers to a highly specific number known to anyone who is familiar with the symbol. If the knowing reaction to π were distorted by subjective, ego-motivated attitudes, that knowledge about π would be considered immature and faulty.

The specific characteristic of logical and conceptual thinking, as Piaget points out, is its tendency towards an intellectual grasp of reality, undistorted by symbolic concomitants or an ego-motivated attitude. Consequently, maturity of logical thinking parallels an increasing liberation of thinking from its symbolic manifestation. A child who considers that the amount of liquid changes when the appearance of the container changes, indicates that for him the intelligent grasp of the concept of "amount" is still tied to an image. When the first operational stage is reached, that image may still be there but it no longer dominates in any way the intellectual grasp, i.e., the child knows that the amount of liquid is not dependent on the image of the container.

It seems to follow that the symbol by itself can not explain the transition from pre-operational to operational thinking. An identical symbol, whether an image or a verbal expression, may be available to and used by the thinking person in the pre-operational and the operational stage. In the first stage, the symbol ties logical thinking to its own subjective and distorting existence. For that reason it makes sense during the pre-operational stage to refer to thinking as taking place "in symbols," "in images," or "in words." At the operational stage, however, these symbols or words may still be present, but their existence is now a concomitant, not a distorting determinant of thinking. Yet even this freedom of logical operations from their symbolic basis does not come about in one stroke. Piaget distinguishes a concrete-operational stage from a formal-operational stage. This latter stage is characterized not so much by greater freedom from symbolic distortion as by greater flexibility in coordinating logical operations. This permits a person to see different possible viewpoints simultaneously and to take into account mutually related logical operations.

As far as the symbol is concerned, in logical thinking it is outer-directed by the very function of intelligence. In other areas of human activity, intelligence is not functioning to minimize subjective and individual experience, merely to guide it. Hence one does not expect a similar freedom or independence of intelligence from the symbolic vehicle in the not-strictly-logical activities of the emotional, social, religious, or artistic sphere. No doubt intelligence is at work, but it works through the symbolic medium, that is, it is partly dependent on it without being thereby immature, as would be the case in logical thinking.

In logical thinking it makes no difference by what specific symbol a concept, e.g., a square, is represented: whether it is an image, or a word, or a movement. The concept of square is not essentially linked to any of these symbols. If it were, the operation would still be partially sensory-motor and consequently immature. In creative art, intelligence transforms a symbolic medium into a representation of an internal state of knowing and feeling. Here it obviously makes a difference whether the representation is in the visual, linguistic or musical medium. The mark of maturity in artistic as against logical thinking does not lie in greater freedom from its symbolic basis.

A Diagram of Thinking Behavior

An attempt is now made to summarize the main points so far covered in this chapter by means of the diagram in Table 15 below. The objective reality to which the organism responds is given in the extreme left column. This may be some physical object or event; in the case of operational intelligence the observable event can be symbolic, for instance in the form of language; while in the case of practical intelligence there can be a stimulus substitute in the form of a signal.

Table 15—Diagram of Thinking Behavior

Objective Reality	Inferred Structure of Operational Intelligence			Manifest Intelligence	Behavioral Observation
	Process	Unit	Object-as-known	Object-as-symbolized	
Physical object, event, or symbol	Perceptual activity	Perception	Perceived present		Verbal report: "I see a tree"
	Operational activity	Concept	Known within a logical framework		Behavior according to a rule or principle. Solution of problem. Inference
	Symbolic activity			Symbol ⎰ outer-directed ⎱ inner-directed	Exchange of linguistic information Image. Ritual
"Practical" Intelligence					
Physical object, event, or signal	Sensory-motor activity	Response, habit	Object-reacted-to	—	Conditioned response. Adaptive action pattern

189

At the extreme right there are samples of observable behavior from which the structure of intelligence is inferred. The inferred structure of operational intelligence forms an undivided whole which for the convenience of the thinking and communicating mind can be arbitrarily broken up into various processes or units. However, in concrete behavior these distinctions break down; a person does not perceive a tree without some operational thinking by which the perception is put within a logical framework, and some concomitant symbolic representation in the imaginative or linguistic medium may also be present.

In terms of abstract units, one can speak of perception or concepts. As was pointed out in Chapter III, one must bear in mind that these units are artificially abstracted from the corresponding thinking activity as if they were the result or the object of this activity. In reality, they are identical with the activity and the abstracted unit, although from a linguistic or philosophical viewpoint one may propose that the source of knowing lies in the structure of intelligence. Thus one can say that perceptual activity results in the object-perceived-as-present or that operational activity results in the object-known-within a logical framework, as long as one understands that neither one nor the other is the object of direct experience. The object-known means the physical object interacting with the person and this interacting *is* the knowing. Only objective behavior, as illustrated in the right-hand column, permits inference to the process of thinking. In reality, perceptual activity = perception = perceived object; just as operational activity = concept = logically known object.

With symbolic activity things are different, since the symbol which is said to result from symbolic activity is an embodiment, hence an objectivation of thinking. The symbol is manifest intelligence and consequently has an objective reality by being tied to a certain medium (motoric, visual, linguistic). While percept or concept can only be considered as abstracted products, symbols are objective products of the intellective process. Symbols result from the structure of intelligence under the aspect of the symbolic activity. They can become true objects of observation, both external and internal.

Insofar as thinking is directed towards internal needs, the resulting symbols can be called inner-directed. On the other side of the continuum are outer-directed symbols which minimize the subjective organismic aspect. Corresponding behavioral samples in the diagram should clarify the distinction between inner and outer-directed although one should realize that in reality this distinction refers to major tendencies and not to an absolute division. Any symbolic behavior manifests some inner-directed and outer-directed components.

Note that the symbol occurs in the left column under objective reality with which intelligence interacts as well as in the column of manifest intelligence, as resulting from intelligence. This double function is characteristic of the symbol and indicates its marvelous ubiquitousness. It is however a major source of possible confusion. If once the symbol is clearly understood as being the direct result of thinking and consequently referring back to its origin, it is obvious that the comprehension of a symbol requires an implicit level of intelligent structure similar to that which originally enabled the production of the symbol. In other words, the symbolic activity is equally at work in the formation of the symbol and in its comprehension.

The lower part of the diagram, in contrast to thinking, concerns what is called practical intelligence, characteristic for the sensory-motor stage of the evolving intelligence. The interaction of organism and physical event is not said to result in an object-known, but in an object-reacted-to. In fact, the observed behavior is identical with practical intelligence. In distinction from thinking behavior, a conditioned response or an action pattern is adequately determined by the physical event and the organism. On this level, signals can function as learned stimulus substitutes.

One may sometimes neglect the symbol-signal distinction at the input side of the organism since the signal in the lower part of the left column corresponds functionally to the symbol in the upper part of that column. However, as the product of intelligence, the symbol has no counterpart at the sensory-motor level.

Function of Language

Language shows in a particularly obvious way the role of the symbol in human intelligence. It is learned through social imitation and incorporated into the young child's behavioral repertoire along with his budding intelligence at the stage of early symbolic manifestations. A young child enjoys the use of language, not as some have thought to practice a linguistic skill but to practice his intellectual grasp of reality. Although it serves in part the purpose of communication, the most important function of language which it shares with play or imagination is in the service of thinking. This is the ego-centric period of Piaget; the period in which internal speech dominates according to Vygotsky.

The slow development of logical thinking indicates rather clearly that language is assimilated to the child's present intel-lectual structure. Most three-year-old children are quite familiar with such words as "some, all, any" and comprehend and use them correctly in simple situations. Yet it is only at a considerably later age that children can firmly grasp the concept of class inclusion and extension. As Inhelder and Piaget (1964, p. 293) point out:

. . . whether a child understands words like "all" and "same," or any other form of words used to refer to the concept of class inclusion and similarity, whether he understands the sort of language we use to refer to the asymmetrical and transitive relation of a series, these are questions which are mainly dependent on the level which he has reached in the development of operational behavior —and that development is relatively independent of any other, because it is governed by its own laws of equilibration. We therefore say that language is not a sufficient and necessary reason for the process.

With language, as with the mental image, or perception, or playful imitation, Piaget is insistent that the symbolic events are not objectively given states which the person passively executes. They are above all manifestations of the internal structure of intelligence; they result from the thinking of the child and can in no way be considered the ready means through which thinking comes about. From the view of the person forming symbols, they should be thought of as end-products of internalized action. To learn to name a thing presupposes the kind of basic knowledge of the permanence of things which was described as object-constancy or object-formation. Once the child has acquired this intellectual skill of regarding objects-as-being-out-there and not merely as objects-to-react-to, then he can assimilate the name to the object-as-known. A name, as such, never supplies the requisite intellectual structure.

From the view of the person comprehending a symbol such as a word, one must also postulate an internalized action which links the symbol to the corresponding state of knowing. Symbols, as distinct from signals, do not work automatically or trigger-off a kind of reflex reaction. Although both man and beast run from a fire, their actions differ as the animal's flight is triggered by a warning signal and man's escape is usually controlled by some form of thinking.

If language cannot explain the beginnings of intelligence, can one at least attribute to language the highest level of formal logical operations? Initially Piaget attempted to contrast formal and concrete thought in terms of a verbal component which must be present in the former. But he continues,

> . . . in spite of appearances and current opinion, the essential characteristic of propositional logic is not that it is a verbal logic. First and foremost, it is a logic of all possible combinations, whether these combinations arise in relation to experimental problems or purely verbal questions . . . the real power of propositional logic lies not in this [verbal] support but rather in the combinational power which makes it possible for reality to be fed into the set of possible hypotheses compatible with the data (Inhelder and Piaget, 1958, p. 253).
> . . . Moreover, the details of verbal expression vary between subjects and sometimes even from moment to moment for a single subject (p. 279).

In other words, Piaget rejects the notion that mature logical thinking finds its explanation or base in the verbal symbol. Whether thinking takes place in response to verbal questions or in objective life situations, whether it is expressed and internally supported by verbal expression or not, is largely irrelevant. The specific aspect of logical thinking resides in the interaction of the thinking person with reality. This interaction is described as an assimilation of reality "into the set of possible hypotheses compatible with the data." The psychologist concerned with thinking should study this set or structure and describe its behavioral characteristics. An investigation of the verbal concomitants which are not formally related to thinking cannot adequately achieve this goal.

In the past, an explanation of concepts—as if they were independently existing objects of thinking—was sought in a person's subjective image, typically in the visual imagination. These images were thought to be blurred and rather vague and thus were considered capable of picturing a kind of general concept into which all possible instances of the concept could be fitted. This viewpoint, which was in all seriousness entertained by leading scholars, is now largely discarded not because of its inherent faulty reasoning on the nature of concept and image, but because it became empirically evident that different people varied tremendously in power of imagination. The fate of the introspective school of psychology and the "imageless thought" controversy documented the futility of tying thinking to images. Apart from the fact that some people are born blind and obviously develop logical thinking and that other ostensibly normal people report that they cannot internally visualize anything, there are just too many concepts in which a translation into pictures is overly arbitrary and entirely forced.

It is here put forward that images or types of imagination do not contribute to a specific understanding of intelligent functioning, except perhaps in some special skills which require visual or auditory representation. It is noteworthy that the growth of logical thinking takes place as well in a blind as in a seeing child, as well in a motionless paralytic as in a child who moves around normally. As far as intellectual skill is concerned, Galton long ago observed no basic difference between a visually gifted person and another person of the so-called kinesthetic type of imagination.

Scholars who attempted to explain thinking in terms of image had it all mapped out in the brain. There were the receptors which gave us sensations and these were combined into perceptions. The perceptions became impressed into the neural structure of the brain and remained there as images which a person could "look at," much as we look at a photo album. For instance, from having seen a great number of different dogs, there eventually emerged the internal picture of a "general" dog and that is the picture a person "looked at" when he thought of the concept of dog. Language learning fitted into this schema rather neatly. The sound sequence "DOG" generated an auditory image of the word. This sound image simply had to be connected to the visual, preferably the generalized visual picture, and thus the child had learned the meaning of the word "dog."

There is no serious scholar today who holds such a simplified "picture" theory. But the great danger is that language or the linguistic symbol is now more and more conceived as substituting in the role which the image played before. On the face of it, language has many advantages over subjective images; it is almost—apart from deaf people—universally present since early childhood; it is objective, in the sense that speaking can be observed and recorded in writing; it is also objective in that it is conceived as localized in specific parts of the brain; and most importantly, a name, by definition, is a generalized concept so that one does not have to resort to the artifact of a "generalized" picture. Yet if one reads a description of the acquisition of logical concepts as sketched by contemporary psychologists who rely on verbal explanations, one realizes that an ill-conceived theory has not become better because it appears more plausible.

Piaget (1960, p. 32) has warned about the fascination that consciousness derives from the ease of verbal thought.

Introspection experiences the greatest difficulty in realizing by its own methods that it is itself an item of behavior; verbal behavior is an action, doubtless scaled down and remaining internal, a rough draft of action which constantly runs the risk of being nothing more than a plan, but it is nevertheless an action, which simply replaces things by signs and movements by their evocation, and continues to operate in thought by means of these spokesmen. Now, introspection, ignoring this active aspect of verbal thought, sees in it nothing but reflection, speech and conceptual representation, which explains the mistaken belief of introspective psychologists that intelligence is reducible to those privileged terminal states, and the delusion of logicians that the most adequate logistic pattern must be essentially a theory of "propositions."

It is important, therefore, in order to arrive at the real functioning of intelligence, to reverse this natural movement of the mind and to revert to thinking in terms of action itself; only in this way will the role of this internal action, the operation, appear in a clear light. And this very fact forces us to recognize the continuity which links operation with true action, the source and medium of intelligence.

As we reflectively introspect and become aware of internal private language during a period of problem solving, we are easily tempted, says Piaget, to conceptualize thinking as a looking-onto an internal screen, or what the philosopher Price (1953) calls a kind of "inspection." Deceived by our own internal evidence, we make internal speech the object of this inspection and identify the verbal symbol with the very process of thinking.

The basic flaw of any theory which attempts to explain thinking in terms of verbal or other symbolic units lies in three false assumptions. One is that concepts are real units of thinking, the other, that concept and symbol, particularly verbal symbol, are identical, and the third, that symbols are transmitted and function like signals or substitute stimuli. Instead of considering the symbolic embodiment of thinking activity, these theories go along with our deceiving introspection and see the symbolized halting places as somehow real and given. Satisfied that symbols are objective, real and in no need of explanation, it is an easy transition to continue in this direction and assume that the symbolic units explain or carry the meaning of the concepts. In this way one ascribes to concepts a reality level that one observes in symbols.

To study thinking one has, as Piaget says, to reverse this natural movement of the mind. Action is the source and medium of intelligence and the reality of concepts must be sought in the action of thinking which can become embodied in a symbolic medium. But human intelligence is neither tied to any particular type of internal images, nor to any particular type of symbols. As the need arises, new words are added to our vocabulary. The human mind is inventive enough to create the symbols that can serve intelligence and human communication.

The phenomenon of deaf children and adolescents without a verbal language should be a source of constant wonderment at the inventive power of the human intellect. We hearing persons have been exposed to the verbal language of our society and can be considered fortunate that ready symbols are supplied to us. These symbols facilitated social communication and provided untold opportunities for information and intellectual curiosity. In such a situation one is so easily inclined to find additional support for the above mentioned theory which ascribes to language the basis of intellectual development.

A common reaction to the evidence for a normal intellectual development in the language-deficient deaf is the question: "If they do think, what do they think *in?*" This question betrays the questioner's theoretical outlook on thinking and language. Deaf people's intelligence can obviously not be explained as due to language, but, as we also see, neither can language explain the intelligent behavior of the hearing. If this question is reinterpreted to ask what types of symbols deaf people create for themselves, we are free to speculate about visual, kinesthetic, and gestural symbols. At the same time we realize that a good part of a hearing child's intellectual growth is also more readily revealed in nonverbal than in verbal symbolism.

Nevertheless, the fact is striking that most deaf children grow up without a ready-made symbol system for communication and hence without that abstract system of symbols by which we refer to concepts. They are largely left to their own devices for communication with others and for internal thinking. The evidence for conceptual thinking in the linguistically deficient deaf has been presented and leads to the direct conclusion that thinking develops through living contact with

198

the environment regardless of the presence or absence of a ready-made linguistic symbol system.

Whether the thinking of linguistically deficient deaf people has ever reached the height of intellectual and creative achievement which is admired in our culture is a moot point. Exceptional achievement presupposes certainly many more factors besides linguistic competence—if that is necessary—and opportunities for intellectual development in the deaf have not been as plentiful as among educated people. Moreover, these few people who were born deaf and achieved some unusual intellectual competence usually master the language of their society. Before one jumps to the unwarranted conclusion that language enabled these deaf to reach uncommon achievement, one should consider the millions and millions of people who in spite of linguistic competence, remain the "common" people. Moreover, one should accept the existence of individual differences ("talent") or inquire into the home or school situation of those few exceptional persons. These environmental situations may have been particularly favorable for general intellectual, including linguistic development. As far as the common deaf or the common hearing is concerned, no large scale investigation has ever discovered any substantial relation between intelligence level and linguistic measurements.

The evidence for this statement is summarized in Table 16 below. This table shows correlations reported in the literature, between linguistic measures and IQ tests of children, aged from 5.5 to 15.5 years, and of retarded youngsters, aged 13 to 21 years. Quite consistently, measures related to linguistic structure show only a very weak positive correlation which stays close to the average of .16 for sentence complexity and IQ, based on all 746 persons. The corresponding average for sentence length, based on N = 426, is .16. Interestingly, articulation has a somewhat stronger association with IQ, as the grand average of .41, based on N = 426, demonstrates.

Table 16—Correlations Between Intelligence and Language Measures

Author	Subjects	N	CA	Length	Complexity	Articulation
Winitz (1959)	Kindergarten	150	5.5	.18	.24	.34
Templin (1957)	Grade School	60	6	.39	.26	.37
		60	7	.08	.00	.39
		60	8	.15	.30	.29
Harrell (1957)	Public School	80	9.5		.17 (.18)*	
		80	11.5		.08 (.28)	
		80	13.5		.08 (.29)	
		80	15.5		.07 (.11)	
Goda and Griffith (1961)	Retarded	96	13–21	.17	.08	.58

* Figures in bracket refer to written language.

Such a result comes as a surprise to workers in the area of intellectual tests and measurement who have consistently noted that verbal tests produce the most reliable IQ scores. However, these verbal tests do not distinguish linguistic competence from intelligent linguistic use. One need only consider that apart from the hearing impaired, all children learn language as long as their intellectual level is above a very low ceiling. Once a person reaches a mental age of four years he can master the natural language to which he is exposed, just as he can master basic perceptual or motoric skills. It is an easily observable fact that under existing conditions children learn language before they learn to tie shoe laces.

Language has aptly been called the best show which man can put on and indeed it stands unquestionably among the highest achievements in the evolutionary scale. Scholars who are attempting to fathom the secret of linguistic competence and usage find that their task requires an understanding of the psychological functioning of the human organism. In this sense mature use of language is the crown of the building, not its foundation. For that reason language cannot be the means by which skills prerequisite to linguistic competence and use are to be explained.

Language as a symbol does not explain; only a signal by

itself explains and determines an action. A symbol as such never explains or determines; it represents a state of knowing and finds its explanation in that knowledge. Signals can be conditioned and directly transmitted. Symbols, however, are spokesmen of an internal knowing and their production and their comprehension hinges on that knowing or thinking activity. To understand a signal we observe the organism's reaction; to understand a symbol we must understand the internal activity of thinking through which a symbol is produced and comprehended.

In this chapter an attempt was made to bring some of Piaget's insights to bear on the compelling problem of how to understand the intellectual development of the deaf. A condition for success in this attempt was the willingness to accept the nonverbal character of deaf people's mental life and to take a theoretical viewpoint on thinking which does not introduce linguistic competence as a necessary explanatory factor. To summarize in a few pages the main tenets of Piaget is a difficult task. The reader whose interest has been aroused is referred to the sources, particularly the one book in which Piaget deals expressly with symbolic behavior. The book, entitled *La Formation du Symbole,* is available to English readers under the subtitle which emphasizes some of the material content rather than the formal purpose of the book: *Play, Dreams and Imitation in Childhood.* The originality of Piaget's view is his discovery of the relation between many essentially nonverbal types of behavior and the intellectual structure which they as symbols reveal. Piaget has never extensively worked with deaf people or given deep attention to the significance of their intellectual development. Thus it would seem that the success of his theory in making sense of deaf people's intellectual functioning is a not insignificant support for the soundness of his theory.

CHAPTER XIV

Practical Implications

Deaf persons have in the past been likened to dumb animals and relegated to the category of the demented. They were considered legally and humanly incompetent. This attitude was based on the assumption that speech is the distinguishing mark of the rational as compared to the irrational animal. What has been primarily responsible for our changed attitude toward the deaf? It was chiefly the discovery that speech could be taught to at least some of the deaf. This empirical fact demonstrated conclusively that deafness is not necessarily connected with lack of intelligence.

Yet today speech or language is still the passport required to admit the deaf into the society of fully developed human beings. At least this is the philosophy underlying our present educational and rehabilitative process. This also is the attitude we inculcate implicitly in parents of deaf children, in society at large and last but not least in the deaf person himself. From this angle, we perceive a certain basic similarity between our present viewpoint and that of past centuries vis-à-vis the deaf. In effect we are still saying to them: "On condition that you learn our language, we are willing to accept you." The principal difference is that while this feat was not considered possible in the past, today it is thought to be the normal and predominant situation among the deaf.

This attitude is constantly nourished by theories of scholars who extol language as the source and medium of civilization and intelligence. One can hardly blame educators and speech therapists if they take their lead from such exponents of learning.

Actually the general failure of the deaf to acquire linguistic competence poses a remarkable challenge, not only to educators, but to scientists. The latter have not seriously investigated this problem and the former are left to attribute the failure in a rather superficial manner to low intelligence, poor teaching methods, minimal brain damage, or to some mysterious law of least effort, according to which children would not learn to walk if we permitted them to crawl!

Here is an instance of what Festinger called cognitive dissonance. On one hand we honestly desire to accept the deaf child and help him attain maturity by the only means at our disposal, namely language. On the other hand, facts demonstrate that the vast majority of the deaf never acquire linguistic competence. Quite obviously the educator is at an impasse. Even apart from the oral-manual controversy which forces all specialists in this field to take sides and puts them on the defensive—certainly not an atmosphere conducive to realistic objective appraisal—what else can the teacher do but insist on more and more language? For language is the only means, he is told, of making the deaf acceptable to our society. As for the facts of the deaf pupil's very limited progress, there is a subtle tendency to suppress them. They are known, of course, but not discussed too openly or too definitely. They are treated like sex in Freud's Vienna. Thus reading norms are published for the deaf, as illustrated in Chapter II, but they are not directly compared to the achievement of hearing children. One hears statements to the effect that the deaf are two or three years behind, or one consoles parents with the small number of words a hearing child in second grade is able to *read,* as though this were comparable to the number of words a deaf child *knows.*

These defense mechanisms are but minor factors in comparison with the potentially harmful effect of our unrealistic attitude on the deaf themselves and their immediate families. If experts are divided, how can the already distraught parent decide among them? If scholars teach that language is the most important factor contributing to intellectual development, how can the ordinary person disagree? If the speech teacher stresses the need for constant unrelenting effort toward oral speech, what parent would still search for nonverbal methods of education for his deaf child?

We cannot forget about the child himself who is given to understand that he will be accepted by his parents and society at large only if he learns language. The primary need for healthy development of any child, particularly one with a disability, is acceptance of himself as a person. This acceptance should not be made conditional on an aspect of behavior directly connected with the child's disability and therefore beyond his control. Such acceptance is rarely accorded deaf children unless they are born to unusual parents. Our educational and scientific atmosphere does not permit us really to accept deafness.

The oral educational philosophy is bound to be detrimental to the relationship of the deaf child to his parents. It is hard for any parent to accept the fact that his child is deaf or otherwise permanently disabled. This particular disability, moreover, unlike some others, usually is diagnosed only after many months or years of anxious doubt, unrealistic hopes, not to mention financial burdens and untold inconveniences. This cannot help but have its effect on the young child to whose already great handicap must be added the burden of doubts about his own worth, as he witnesses his parents' distress and feels his isolation from other family members.

Those guiding the education of the deaf child impress very early on the parents' mind the all-importance of the speech and language factor. To my knowledge hearing parents of deaf children are never encouraged to learn the sign language of the deaf. Thus the deaf child and his parents, directed to stress speech and lip reading and discouraged from using manual signs, are left to their own devices in communicating with one another. Many parents try faithfully, in what they believe is their child's best interest, to follow the teacher's advice. Meantime, the child is growing and reaches the age of five or six years. The level of communication of which he is capable by means of speech is of the most primitive type, hardly above the signals by which we communicate with our pets. The child implicitly understands that his parents and the hearing society they represent will not love him as he is, but will accept him only if he learns speech. Thus he is deprived of the unconditional acceptance that is the foundation of normal healthy development for any child.

By the time the child enters school the battle for mastery of language is already largely lost. The child's intelligence has been developing without benefit of language. He now spends years and years in school, constantly exposed to formal linguistic training, and progressing at a snail's pace to that almost inevitable ceiling of Grade 3 reading level. He is still below the level that would enable him readily to form and comprehend connected language.

However, at the same time, in school he meets for the first time other children like himself, playmates and friends who accept him without requiring verbal language. Outside of class hours he learns to socialize with other children and to communicate in his own way. The large residential schools, willingly or unwillingly, become for most deaf children a substitute for society and family. Many parents recognize this when after years of vain attempts to reach their child through language, they are relieved to see him in congenial surroundings.

Helped by the presence of companions and by the extra-classroom activity provided by the school, most deaf adolescents make a remarkable adjustment in the face of what must surely be considered heavy odds. They have not learned the language society has so insistently foisted upon them, but they consider that the failure lies with society, not with them. The deaf adult exhibits a certain hostility toward the hearing world which may offend our sensibility and good will. Yet is this not an almost unavoidable reaction by which the deaf individual upholds his dignity and counteracts the devaluatory attitude of society? If the deaf person unhesitatingly accepted society's norms, he would have to consider himself less of a person for not having language. The American who is deaf is rightly proud of his independence and his status as a responsible citizen and is unwilling to accept an inferior status of dependency. This is in contrast to the situation of the deaf in other countries and of persons with other disabilities such as blindness, who for reasons not pertinent to this discussion are unfortunately more ready to accept the false standard of society and consequently their own dependency.

Perhaps the linguistic failure of the deaf becomes more understandable when one realizes the irony of our position in wanting to accept deafness but not accepting deficiency in language. To say that the deaf associate experiences of frustration and failure with formal language learning is to understate the case. Yet no failing experience interferes with a hearing child's acquisition of language. The following statement is admittedly speculation but it is in accord with all we know about the psychology of language acquisition: The deaf child fails to acquire language because it is taught too late, in an unreasonable medium, in an unnatural way, and by the wrong person.

206

The biologically appropriate time for learning a first language is before the age of 3 or 3.5, during the period when the infant's intelligence blossoms in symbol formation. While scholars may be impressed by the fact that some deaf children can acquire linguistic competence at a considerably later age, I am willing to note these as exceptions and accept the biological norm. Then too, it is unreasonable to expect deaf children to learn by means of visible lip movements alone. Lip movements are inadequate even for the best of lip readers who must fill in large gaps in the visible information by educated guesses and intellectual effort. A more easily discriminable method seems absolutely necessary. Thirdly, the very idea of giving formal teaching before one can communicate informally with a child is contrary to the child's psychological status. Children learn admirably when the learning serves a psychological function and becomes incorporated into their thinking structure, but formal learning—divorced from informal communication—is quite foreign much before the age of eight and rarely leads to lasting success.

Finally, children should acquire their first language in the environment in which they make the first giant steps in the intellective and symbolic grasp of reality. A late beginning in learning language necessarily divorces the learning of the first means of communication from the learning of specific social and emotional reactions to significant persons in their immediate society.

It is a rather sad commentary on the present educational situation that the example of Soviet Russia was required before any attempt to introduce manual spelling at an early age became acceptable in American schools for the deaf. This is a measure of the appeal of an ideal deaf person, one whose oral behavior would not betray his deafness any more than his outward appearance gives a clue as to his inability to hear. This ideal not only insisted on linguistic competence but on speech expression and speech reception as well. Manual spelling is English language. Yet any school introducing this method with small children ten years ago would have been forced to abandon this method as not sufficiently "oral."

One important reason for the dominance of the oral method may be mentioned. Some eighty years ago when the oral method began to assert itself and quickly became predominant in all schools for the deaf, the picture of the deaf population in these schools was quite different from what it is today. Oralism could never have gained such impetus if the majority of deaf children had come to school then as they do now without any linguistic competence. Thanks to modern medicine acquired deafness after the age of early language acquisition is now rare. But quite the opposite situation prevailed eighty years ago, or even thirty years ago. Then most of the pupils at schools for the deaf had lost their hearing after the age of natural language acquisition. Hence, most of the deaf knew their mother tongue before they became deaf and with these deafened persons it made sense to insist so strongly on preserving speech and learning lip reading.

Today there are only a handful of deafened children. The greatest need of the deaf child now is not speech but language, and it is only by a distortion of its original purpose that the oral method holds sway as the ordinary and preferred way of acquiring linguistic competence.

Yet as the oral method has now, for better or worse, reached its dominant position in the education of the deaf, the presence of even one profoundly deaf student who succeeds well by the oral method is sufficient to insure its continued prevalence. This permits educators to point to their outstanding pupils as living arguments in support of the pure oral approach. To others this is very much like singling out Paderewski and Horowitz to a parent and saying: "Look how well they play the piano! If they can do it, why not your child?"

The so-called oral-manual controversy in the education of the deaf is not really a controversy that can be settled on its

208

practical merit since there is no such thing as a truly manual education. One can read compromise statements which reflect the thinking of many educators, such as: "All deaf children must first be given the opportunity of an oral education. If by age twelve they show little sign of success, one may use manual methods of education." One wonders whether any thought at all is being given to the developing mind of the twelve year old child. The fixation on the one secondary aspect of language, namely speech, in preference to everything else, including linguistic competence, is indeed baffling. This oral preoccupation must strike a neutral observer as irrational. It is like some strange custom or institution which is encouraged within a community although perceived as harmful by an outsider.

Even learning one's mother tongue through manual spelling in a formal school setting at five years of age as is now practiced in a few schools, is too late and too unnatural a procedure to result in general success. At that age, the effort is already remedial learning rather than first language learning. A wise educator of the deaf once remarked that the more intelligent deaf child may be hindered by his very intelligence from acquiring verbal language. By this he implied that linguistic competence is rooted in the beginnings of intellectual life as an acquired symbolic medium and frame of social expression. If society does not provide the child with conventional symbols, he can still develop intellectually, but the symbol system which embodies his thinking will be different from the verbal system, so much so that the two systems may be actively opposed.

Perhaps we could learn much about that private symbol system of the deaf if we were content to study their manual signing in an objective fashion without comparing it to the "mature" verbal language of our society and calling it by contrast "primitive" and "concrete." Apart from this it would seem to be a most significant fact, worthy of scientific atten-

209

tion, that signing is learned by practically all the deaf while the verbal language is mastered by only a few.

The additional general observation can be made that all infants learn any language to which they are exposed in a natural way during the first three years, provided the important sensory cues are transmitted and internally processed. It would seem to follow quite logically that a deaf child too could learn society's language in an almost infallible way. If parents were taught to make a discriminable sign for each word while they speak it, this procedure would almost necessarily teach the deaf child the natural language. In this manner the deaf child would come to use signs in the same way in which we use morphemes and the transition from these signs to written English would be a matter of transliteration rather than translation. That is, the child would sign according to the English syntax, not according to the popular sign language in common use. Thus the greatest obstacle to learning English would be removed because deaf children would already have learned to comprehend and express themselves in English syntax. Comprehension of syntactical rules, it will be recalled, rather than memory of single words, is currently the great obstacle which so few deaf children learn to overcome.

Objections to this proposal may invoke the idea of least effort: "Children permitted to use a manual, easily discriminable form of communication will not be motivated to work at the arduous task of receptive and expressive speech." Even though this argument is patently fallacious, it is hard to see how one could prefer a situation in which 90 per cent of the deaf do not know language and perhaps 4 per cent are excellent in both aspects of speech, to a situation in which 90 per cent of the deaf conceivably would have linguistic competence and possibly only 3 per cent would be proficient speech artists.

A second objection is somewhat more serious. Does signing according to English syntax exist, and would parents be willing to use it? As to the last point, I am convinced that parents, once they are made to understand the real situation, will be cooperative, just as in the past they listened to other advice. Besides, there does not seem to be any other way in which parents can demonstrate to their deaf child that they accept him and are willing to communicate with him on his own terms. Such parents would not anxiously base their hopes on the slender chance of an unlikely event. They would enjoy living contact with the child who needs only to be exposed to discriminable cues to pick up language like any other normal child. The signing which is proposed would not be as difficult to learn as a foreign language. It would be English in which frequently used words or morphemes would have simple, gesture-like signs. Some spelling would obviously be necessary and some manual signs for syntactical features now completely neglected in the conventional sign language would have to be devised.

Use of such manual signs, in addition to encouraging the learning of English linguistic structure, would also actually enhance the use of speech or hearing aids. The need for symbolic imitation and comprehension is so strong that a two-year-old child will not voluntarily neglect any cues which would facilitate meaningful symbolic communication. An additional benefit of this suggested program would be a possible insight into the perplexing problem of so-called "aphasic" children, i.e., children whose hearing sensitivity is presumed to be adequate but who cannot make use of the sounds they apparently "hear." If there is a cerebral center which mediates linguistic behavior, would truly aphasic children be separated from deaf children by the fact that they cannot learn to *sign* the English language?

These considerations concerning a realistic program of teaching language to the deaf were prompted by a survey of

211

the present situation prevailing throughout the modern world and a more adequate scientific description of the natural development of thinking and language as outlined in previous chapters. A more direct application of conclusions derived from experimental work on the thinking of the deaf is the need to question seriously our educational method which stresses and relies almost exclusively upon verbal skill. Tradition has been rather heavily loaded with educational disciplines deriving their existence from linguistic habits. We need only look back over endless controversies which today strike us as semantic follies. Perhaps such emphasis could be condoned as long as education was limited to the few presumed to be sophisticated in their use of language. But with the development of free and compulsory education for all, some of the verbal rigor was relaxed and an increase in the use of audio-visual and other concrete aids have become common. Yet in spite of these liberalizing trends, the basic tendency to equate scholastic learning with verbal learning is still very much in evidence.

Underlying this general emphasis on verbal learning was the ready association of thinking and language which prevailed in one form or another throughout the history of Western thought and education. The history of the deaf stands out as one exceptionally glaring instance of man's inability to see beyond the confines of his own theoretical assumptions. The evidence brought together in these pages is not intended to devaluate language or displace it from its legitimate place in the education of verbal persons, but to clear the way for a scientific appreciation of the thinking process upon which verbal learning should take place.

The amount of unthinking verbal learning in our schools at every grade level from kindergarten to university is still vast. For every student who thinks clearly and has difficulty communicating his thought verbally, there are easily a hundred others who say things they have not thought through. Such use of linguistic behavior is expected in ordinary conversation or routine everyday life, but it plays havoc with an education which purports to train thinking.

Leaving the general educational situation aside, society is still faced with great numbers of children who for one reason or another are deficient, not in linguistic competence as the deaf are, but in various linguistic skills. There are the millions of mentally retarded, the millions of culturally deprived, the emotionally disturbed, and the children with articulation disorders, or reading difficulties. All these and other children with linguistic deficiencies pose special educational problems. We admit such children are particularly deficient in linguistic behavior and then, as if to punish them for this, we focus our educational curriculum on their weakest point.

How many hours are wasted because instructions are framed in a verbal medium whose linguistic meaning baffles the child so that he does not even come to the point of considering the subject matter under discussion? How can thinking ensue from the recognition of a problem if the message does not get through and the real problem is the linguistic obstacle of comprehending the message? In a similar vein, many wrong verbal answers reveal a lack of verbal skill more than a lack of thinking.

These points are particularly pertinent at the younger age levels, before the child's intelligence in operational thinking frees him from too exclusive a dependence on specific symbolic representations and on perceptually present situations. If at this level linguistic skill is not firmly established, the child will be particularly handicapped by the fact that language symbols are not readily transformed into representational images. A deaf child's failure to solve the verbal problem which asks for the way in which "thermometer" and "scales" are alike is simply due to his ignorance of the key words, as

213

well as of their syntactical connection. A child somewhat lacking in linguistic skill for various reasons may be so preoccupied with the effort to comprehend the verbal message that the relevant thinking to produce the common concept and its corresponding verbal term does not even take place. The study by Furth and Milgram (1965) reported in Chapter VII isolated conceptual from linguistic components in this kind of task and demonstrated that educable retarded children fall behind on such tasks for lack of verbal skill rather than lack of conceptual thinking.

Just as linguistic competence cannot be drilled into the growing deaf child, ineptness in linguistic usage cannot be remedied by constant exposure to formal verbal teaching. On the contrary, the net effect of such a procedure is to make formal teaching even more distasteful to the child, widening the gulf between language and the development of thinking. For children in any way deficient in linguistic usage, educational procedures should concentrate on the stronger part of their intellectual structure, not exclusively on verbal means.

This plea for nonverbal teaching methods is no longer completely novel, as is demonstrated by the recent upsurge of interest in the Montessori method, and by new teaching methods for mathematics which practically eliminate verbal language. The need for letting children discover principles of thinking through activity is now frequently mentioned.

If educators firmly accepted the notion that thinking is first and foremost doing, acting, behaving, or internally operating rather than just knowing the right word, and if they agreed that education should primarily teach and develop thinking according to a child's optimal potential, they would more readily seek nonverbal teaching methods, particularly in cases where linguistic skill is retarded or absent.

At the Center for Research in Thinking and Language, we are currently planning a course in thinking, a nonverbal training curriculum for discovery, inference, conceptual control, transfer, symbolic transformation and combination, to be given to deaf or otherwise linguistically handicapped children. Its purpose will be to develop thinking skills in pupils otherwise exposed to practically no formal educational training except rote memory of linguistic symbols. The advantages of such a procedure are obvious and manifold, and many educators have expressed their interest in cooperating with it.

Not least among the fruits of such an endeavor would be a clearer insight into the actual intellectual potential of linguistically handicapped persons. In general we have been satisfied to point out what they could not do. The experimental studies reported here, however, are but an indication that thinking is going on in the linguistically handicapped deaf. To study the limits of this thinking and to observe more closely its processes and strategies necessitate that the psychologist venture into training and education.

A Teaching Demonstration of Logical Thinking with Deaf Children*

It seems fitting to end the present investigation of the thinking processes of deaf people with a report on a short teaching session in logical thinking with classes of ten deaf pupils each at three age levels, 9, 13, and 18 years. On four consecutive days classes were seen for about 40 minutes and on the last day all pupils took a test.

The idea of employing the method of symbolic logic was previously explored in connection with the experiment on

---

* A demonstration film is available from U.S. Office of Education, *Captioned Films for the Deaf*, Washington, D.C. 20202.

215

Logical Symbol Use and Discovery. But now the experiment was turned into a training session in which an entire class participated, and repeated examples, discoveries and corrections were feasible.

The teacher started by putting the following on the blackboard:

$$H \rightarrow \text{⌂}$$

then he asked the class to fill in the missing symbol in

$$? \rightarrow \text{♀}$$

The children quickly caught on that a letter

$$T$$

can symbolize an object (tree) and put down S or M for

☆   and   ♀

respectively.

Then the teacher indicated the meaning of a straight bar over the symbol by the natural gesture for "no" and the children were shown that

$$\bar{H} \rightarrow \text{♀}$$

or

$$\overline{T} \rightarrow \text{☆}$$

Now the following was put on the blackboard:

$$S \rightarrow \text{⌂}$$

The children observing the error, were prompted to correct this in one of three ways: 1) by putting a negation over the S:

$$\bar{S} \rightarrow \text{⌂}$$

216

2) by crossing out the arrow:

$$S \nrightarrow \text{⌂}$$

or 3) by adding a star to the house:

$$S \rightarrow \text{⌂} \quad ☆$$

In this manner the children by nonverbal discovery began to comprehend a number of important rules of thinking. They learned implicitly that the symbol on the left side of the expression represents the affirmation of a concept, a mental product; that the picture on the right side stands for objective reality and that the arrow indicates a judgment of truth or falsehood. Thus H stands for the proposition "There exists a house," and the arrow pointing to the pictured house indicates the truth of the statement. One could also say that H symbolizes the generalized class of house, that the arrow means "is exemplified by" and that the picture is a valid instance of the class as symbolized on the left.

The negation sign, meant to negate the symbol under it, generates either a sentence of the kind: "There is no house" or the class of "Non-house" both of which are exemplified by anything that is not a house, e.g., a tree. The children are shown that the "null class" or "nothing" is a correct instance of a negation, e.g.,

$$\overline{H} \rightarrow 0.$$

Moreover, they learn that the sequence

$$\overline{H} \rightarrow \text{Q}$$

is identical to

$$H \nrightarrow \text{Q}$$

that is, the affirmation of a negated sentence is identical to the negation of the affirmed sentence.

217

Furthermore, the children observed that the multiplication of additional or other instances does not invalidate a given symbolic sentence or conceptual class:

$$H \rightarrow \text{⬆}$$

and

$$H \rightarrow \text{⬆} \text{⬆}$$

and

$$H \rightarrow \text{⬇} \text{⬆} \text{✷}$$

The latter example relates to the logical principle of simplification which says that it is no falsehood to state the presence of only one element in a given situation containing more elements.

Subsequently, the logical connectives of conjunction and exclusive disjunction were introduced by putting symbolic sentences on the board and by using some simple gestures. This sample shows a conjunction in which the presence of both parts of the conjunction is required:

$$T \cdot H \rightarrow \text{⬆} \text{⬇}.$$

In distinction, with an exclusive disjunction, the presence of only one of the alternatives is required, while the presence of both or neither is incorrect. The following example shows how exclusive disjunction was demonstrated:

$$H/T \rightarrow \left\{ \begin{matrix} \text{⬆} \\ \text{⬇} \end{matrix} \right., \quad H/T \nrightarrow \text{⬇} \text{⬆}.$$

Further combinations of negation, conjunction or disjunction were employed. For the instance,

$$\bar{H} \cdot T \rightarrow ?$$

where the teacher asked for one instance only, the correct drawing was

$$\text{⬇}$$

218

What would be the correct instance after

$$\bar{H} \cdot \bar{T} \rightarrow ?$$

On this, as in other examples, children began to learn flexibility in thinking and observed the difference between a logically required and a logically possible instance. There are many different correct instances to a given concept, just as there are also different ways in which to conceptualize a given situation.

A first answer to

$$\bar{H} \cdot \bar{T} \rightarrow ?$$

was usually something like

This was correct, but it seemed to indicate that the children were inclined to make a one by one match instead of recognizing that zero or one or three or any number or instances would be correct, as long as a house and a tree were absent. To counteract this tendency, the teacher asked for several alternatives in the following manner:

Similarly, when asked to complete

the only certain affirmative symbol was T and any symbol except T could be negated. Here is an example of correct symbolizations that were possible for the given instance of a tree:

$$T, \bar{H}, T \cdot \bar{S}, T/S, \bar{H} \cdot \bar{S}.$$

The teaching proceeded one step further in negation by placing the negation bar over the logical connectives. Thus $\dot{\div}$ or $\not{/}$ would mean the denial of the conjunction or of the exclusive disjunction, respectively. Would nine-year-old children understand the difference between

$$\bar{H} \cdot \bar{T}$$

and

$$H \dotdiv T$$

Would they comprehend that

$$\bar{H} \cdot \bar{T} \nrightarrow ⌂$$

but

$$H \dotdiv T \rightarrow ⌂$$

Could they grasp that

$$\bar{H} \cdot T \rightarrow ⚥$$

but

$$\bar{H}/T \rightarrow ⚥ ⌂$$

This last example of a disjunctive combination of "a negated house or an affirmed tree" could be verified by other instances, but if a tree is posited and thus one alternative of the disjunction is given, the other alternative must be denied; however, the only way to deny a negated class is to posit it:

$$\bar{H} \nrightarrow ⌂$$

On the fourth day the deaf children were given the same task as criterion task III and VI of the Symbol Use experiment in Chapter X, except that only form instances were used. A group procedure was administered. A sheet with 32 items was handed out and a subject's response was to write between the given symbol and the given instance an arrow $\rightarrow$ or a crossed arrow $\nrightarrow$.
Figure 7, p. 142, illustrates an item for each of the different operations tested. This test resulted in the distribution of successful subjects in each operation as shown in Figure 9.

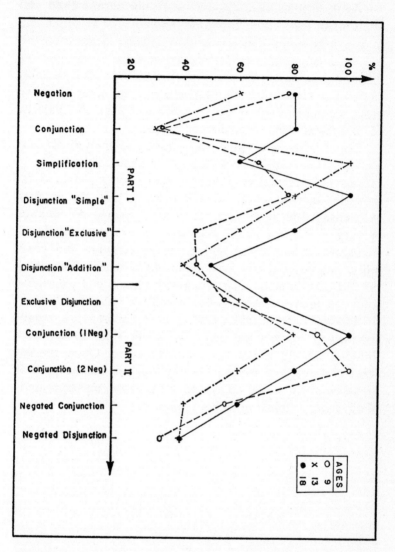

Figure 9. Percentage of successful subjects at three age levels on different logical operations in the final test.

221

As three trials were given for each operation a child who was correct on at least two trials was counted as successful. It should be noted that the symbol and the instance on this test were not as clearly distinct as were the letters and the pictures given during the class period. This difference probably caused some confusion. Nevertheless, one can observe that on most operations even at the youngest age level, the majority of youngsters demonstrated some success.

The children were quite enthusiastic and enjoyed the class sessions. Here was an opportunity for them to think and to express their mental operations without being penalized for linguistic incompetence. It was obvious that the children were engaged in the business of thinking clearly. All children in varying degrees made judgments of truth or falsehood, distinguished affirmation and negation, certainty and possibility, mental concepts from objective instances. They took the initiative in suggesting symbols, instances and alternative solutions, made corrections and asked for reasons.

During their formal teaching deaf children are usually confined to the rote learning of linguistic skills so that such thinking activity is not frequently observed. Quite possibly other children too, whether or not they are handicapped in linguistic skills, would enjoy and benefit from an opportunity of engaging in thinking without language.

CHAPTER XV

Summary and Conclusions

The following twelve points state in summary fashion the more important theoretical and practical conclusions of this work. They span a wide spectrum of issues and to treat each point exhaustively could become the work of a life time.

When the author started working with the deaf ten years ago he hardly foresaw that the single question: "What do the deaf think *in?*" would lead to such far-reaching implications. Even as tentative answers are found, new questions arise. It appears that the value of a scientific work may not be so much in definite answers to present problems as in relevant questions for future investigations.

1. To speak clearly about the mutual relation of thinking and language it is imperative to distinguish three terms: thinking, symbol, and language. Language is here taken in the strict sense of the natural oral language of a society. Linguistic behavior is that human activity which objectively assumes linguistic competence, e.g., comprehension of speech or reading, meaningful speech, etc. Symbolic behavior implies the presence of a symbol as defined in point 3. Thinking be-

havior is any human activity insofar as it can be considered under the aspect of intelligent adaptation.

2. As has been suggested by Piaget, thinking first becomes manifest in the formation of a stable objective world. Perception of "objects-as-known-out-there" contrasts with the practical intelligence of the sensory-motor stage of adaptation which only knows "things-to-react-to." The differentiation of the self among the objects "out there" in the world is a correlate of this primary step in the evolving intelligence.

3. Corresponding to objects-to-react-to are substitute-objects or signals which elicit a determined reaction according to a learned or species-specific pattern. As the object-to-react-to is objectively given, so is the signal. The correlate of objects-as-known is the symbol and is produced and in turn comprehended by the same intelligent structure which formed the object-as-known. A substitute signal refers to a physical object or event, a symbol to the thinking of a person. A symbol represents and embodies the thinking and is thus an exterior event or, at least, an objectively experienced internal event. All thinking activity which is directly concerned with events not perceptually present employs symbols. Symbols serve to broaden the scope of intelligent adaptation across time and place.

4. Intelligent thinking is inner-directed when it results in symbolic behavior which is dominated by subjectively motivated states. This "symbolic" behavior in the narrow sense contrasts with outer-directed thinking aimed at an objective adaptation to reality. Outer-directed thinking must minimize the subjective state of the person, otherwise thinking is immature or distorted. The conventional language of society can serve this purpose readily. Logical and scientific thinking is the mature stage of outer-directed thinking while creative art and socially developed rites symbolize mature stages of inner directed thinking.

5. Logical thinking develops gradually from its first mani-

224

festation in object-formation around age one to the first evidence of logical operations at age six. In this period of transition pre-logical thinking is tied to perceptual presentation or symbolic representation. As logical thinking develops there is an increased freedom from the internal symbolic event with decreasing degrees of immaturity or distorting ego-centrism. The operational stage is reached when thinking is no longer inherently based on specific symbols, though symbols may be present as concomitant activity. At the formal operational level, thinking is "abstract" precisely because it is not tied to a symbolic representation of a perceptual event but can deal freely with possibilities and their combination.

6. One must counteract the tendency to explain thinking in terms of introspection or by analogy with visual perception. Thinking is not a passive state, a mere looking at concepts but an activity which is functionally analogous to the exterior activity of sensory-motor or practical intelligence. A concept is not the object of the logical operation and cannot be objectively experienced. In itself, the concept lacks any objective reality; it is identical with the logical operation and the object-as-known. It is an artificial end-product which our self-awareness and language grasps and treats as if it were a separate object from thinking. The verbal name given to a concept symbolizes the logical operation. This name can become the object of self-reflection and can serve the purpose of communication.

The false analogy of comparing thinking with visual perception is doubly inappropriate because perception too, as stated in point 2, is merely a label for the end-product of a thinking activity. Finally, any actual thinking is not an isolated bit of behavior, but manifests an internal structure of knowing according to the level of intelligence. A solitary logical operation is a contradiction because of the interrelatedness of intelligent operations.

7. Language is a ready-made conventional symbol system

225

assimilated by the intelligence according to its structure. First-language learning takes place during the time of early symbol formation and is mastered by the time a child is four years old. This mastery is referred to as linguistic competence and must be distinguished from the more or less intelligent use of language.

8. According to points 1, 3, 5, and 7 there can be thinking or conceptual behavior without symbols, e.g., a person observing "perceptually" that A is bigger than B and B bigger than C infers "conceptually" that A is bigger than C. No symbol need be postulated. The presence of a symbol, however, always implies some form of thinking behavior. Explanation of thinking by means of a hypothetical mediating response does not by itself imply the presence of a symbol.

9. It follows that a relation between language and operational thinking is not essential and is not specifically required during the developmental stage. Some symbols are required during the representational phase of thinking and to set the stage for operational thinking, i.e., to communicate and recognize the symbolized elements of a problem. The experimental evidence from linguistically incompetent deaf persons confirms the theoretical postulation for the non-necessity of language.

10. The deaf illustrate some of the effects of linguistic deficiency.

    (a) As a direct result of linguistic incompetence, the deaf fail or are poor on all tasks which are specifically verbal or on a few nonverbal tasks in which linguistic habits afford a direct advantage.

    (b) As an indirect result of linguistic incompetence the deaf are frequently experientially deficient:

        (1) They do not know facts; they lack information.

(2) They exhibit a minimal degree of intellectual curiosity.

(3) They have less opportunity and training to think.

(4) They are insecure, passive, or rigid in unstructured situations.

Some of these effects are more notable at younger age levels and disappear altogether in adulthood.

(c) Apart from these listed effects, the basic development and structure of the intelligence of the deaf in comparison with the hearing is remarkably unaffected by the absence of verbal language. One can reasonably assume that the major area in which the deaf appear to be different from the hearing is in variables related to personality, motivation and values. If substantial differences are found, they will likely be due to experiential and social factors of home, school and the deaf community.

11. The experiential deficiency noted above is tied to linguistic incompetence, but it is proposed that this outcome would be avoidable if nonverbal methods of instruction and communication were encouraged both at home in the earliest years and in formal school education. Some degree of linguistic deficiency and results of linguistic deficiency are present in children other than the deaf, e.g., mentally retarded. A clearer perspective about the primary purpose of education, coupled with the realization that verbal language is not essential for thinking, should lead to significant and advantageous changes in educational methods and content.

12. Formal language learning for deaf children beginning after the age of four is remedial at best and no general success can be expected. Success may be attained only if parents of deaf children, encouraged by experts in the field, face the fact

of deafness and accept the deaf child on his own terms. That is, in case of insufficient hearing parents must have recourse to distinguishable signs and use these together with speech. Practically all deaf children, instead of the present ten per cent, could then be expected to reach a basic competence in English, just as all hearing children in any society learn the language to which they are exposed.

As a final conclusion, the major significance of the reported findings for theories of thinking is the demonstration that logical, intelligent thinking does not need the support of a symbolic *system,* as it exists in the living language of society. Thinking is undoubtedly an internal system, a hierarchical ordering within the person of his interaction with the world. The symbol system of language mirrors and in a certain way expresses that internal organization. However, the internal organization of intelligence is not dependent on the language system; on the contrary, comprehension and use of the ready-made language is dependent on the structure of intelligence.

One would not be justified in asserting that the deaf children who were tested in this study had a symbolic system available to them. Most of them were unfamiliar with the verbal language of society and only poorly acquainted with the manual sign language. Yet, they succeeded on tasks of thinking and quite likely produced symbols if and when they were needed. Whatever system or intellectual ordering of experience was manifest in their behavior was entirely due to their internal structure of thinking and could not conceivably be ascribed to a non-existing symbolic system.

If then the thinking processes of the deaf can and must be explained without recourse to language, a nonverbal approach to thinking may be a fruitful one for studying thinking in general. Through a nonverbal approach one may succeed better in avoiding the pitfalls of introspection and in breaking the limitations imposed by unanalyzed philosophical assumptions. In short, one may thus come closer to the behavioral ideal of an objective study of thinking that is not beclouded by extraneous factors of language and in turn, one may achieve a clearer understanding of the function of language in its relation to thinking.

REFERENCES

Bartlett, F. C. *Remembering. A study in experimental and social psychology.* Cambridge: Cambridge University Press, 1932.

Bartlett, F. C. *Thinking. An experimental and social study.* London: Unwin University Press, 1958.

Bobrove, P. Adjustment to auditory disability in adolescence. Unpublished dissertation, University of Rochester, 1964.

Bruner, J. S. The course of cognitive growth. *Amer. psychologist,* 1964, *19,* 1–15.

Chomsky, N. Explanatory models in linguistics. In E. Nagel, P. Suppes and A. Tarski (Eds.), *Logic, methodology and philosophy of science: Proceedings of the 1960 International Congress.* Stanford: Stanford University Press, 1962.

Furfey, P. H. and Harte, T. J. Interaction of deaf and hearing in Frederick County, Maryland. Studies from The Bureau of Social Research, Catholic University of America, No. 3, 1964.

Furth, H. G. The influence of language on the development of concept formation in deaf children. *J. abnorm. soc. psychol.,* 1961, *63,* 386–389.

Furth, H. G. Classification transfer with disjunctive concepts as a function of verbal training and set. *J. psychol.,* 1963, *55,* 447–485 (a).

Furth, H. G. Conceptual discovery and control on a pictorial part-whole task as a function of age, intelligence, and language. *J. educ. psychol.,* 1963, *54,* 191–196 (b).

Furth, H. G. Conservation of weight in deaf and hearing children. *Child develpm.,* 1964, *35,* 143–150 (a).

Furth, H. G. Conceptual performance in deaf adults. *J. abnorm. soc. psychol.*, 1964, *69*, 676–681 (b).

Furth, H. G. and Mendez, R. A. The influence of language and age on *Gestalt* laws of perception. *Amer. J. psychol.*, 1963, *76*, 74–81.

Furth, H. G. and Milgram, N. A. The influence of language on classification: A theoretical model applied to normal, retarded, and deaf children. *Genet. psychol. monogr.*, 1965, *72*, 317–351.

Furth, H. G. and Youniss, J. Color-object paired-associates in deaf and hearing children with and without response competition. *J. consult. psychol.*, 1964, *28*, 224–227.

Furth, H. G. and Youniss, J. The influence of language and experience on discovery and use of logical symbols. *Brit. J. psychol.*, 1965, *56*.

Galton, T. Inquiries into human faculty and its development. New York: Macmillan, 1883.

Goda, S. and Griffith, B. C. Spoken language of adolescent retardates and its relation to intelligence, age, and anxiety. *Child develpm.*, 1962, *33*, 489–498.

Harrell, L. E. A comparison of the development of oral and written language in school-age children. *Child develpm. monogr.*, 1957, *22*.

Head, H. *Aphasia and kindred disorders of speech*. Cambridge: Cambridge University Press, 1926.

Humphrey, G. *Thinking. An introduction to its experimental psychology*. New York: Wiley, 1963.

Inhelder, Bärbel and Piaget, J. *The growth of logical thinking from childhood to adolescence*. New York: Basic Books, 1958.

Inhelder, Bärbel and Piaget, J. *The early growth of logic in the child*. New York: Harper & Row, 1964.

James, W. *The principles of psychology*. New York: Dover, 1950.

Kendler, Tracy S. and Kendler, H. H. Reversal and nonreversal shifts in kindergarten children, *J. exp. psychol.*, 1959, *58*, 56–60.

Kreezer, G. and Dallenbach, K. M. Learning relation of opposition. *Amer. J. psychol.*, 1929, *41*, 432–441.

Langer, Susanne, K. *Philosophy in a new key. A study in the symbolism of reason, rite, and art*. New York: New American Library, A Mentor Book, 1964.

230

Lovell, K. and Ogilvie, E. A. A study of the conservation of weight in the junior school child. *Brit. J. educ. psychol.*, 1961, *31*, 138–144.

Luria, A. R. *The role of speech in the regulation of normal and abnormal behavior*. London: Pergamon, 1961.

Luria, A. R. and Yudovich, F. I. *Speech and the development of mental processes in the child*. London: Staples, 1959.

Milgram, N. A. and Furth, H. G. The influence of language on concept attainment in educable retarded children. *Amer. J. mental defic.*, 1963, *67*, 733–739.

Morris, C. W. *Signs, language and behavior*. New York: Prentice-Hall, 1946.

Mowrer, O. H. *Learning theory and the symbolic processes*. New York: Wiley, 1960.

Myklebust, H. and Brutten M. A study of the visual perception of deaf children. *Acta oto-laryngol.*, Stockholm, 1953, *105*.

Ogden, C. K. and Richards, I. A. *The meaning of meaning. A study of the influence of language upon thought and of the science of symbolism*. New York: Harcourt, Brace, 1956.

Oléron, P. *Recherches sur le développement mental des sourds-muets*. Paris: Centre National de la Recherche Scientifique, 1957.

Oléron, P. and Herren, H. L'acquisition des conservations et le language: Etude comparative sur des enfants sourds et entendants. *Enfance*, 1961, *14*, 203–219.

Olsson, J. E. and Furth, H. G. Visual memory span in the deaf. *Amer. J. psychol.*, in press.

Osgood, C. E. *Method and theory in experimental psychology*. New York: Oxford University Press, 1953.

Piaget, J. *Psychology of intelligence*. Paterson, New Jersey: Littlefield, Adams, 1960.

Piaget, J. *Play, dreams and imitation in childhood*. New York: Norton, 1962.

Price, H. H. *Thinking and experience*. Cambridge: Harvard University Press, 1953.

Pufall, P. B., Double alternation behavior as a function of age and language. Unpublished Master's thesis, Catholic University of America, 1965.

Rainer, J. D., Altshuler, K. Z., Kallmann, F. J. and Deming, W. E. *Family and mental health problems in a deaf population*. New York: N.Y. State Psychiatric Institute, 1963.

231

Russell, J. Reversal and nonreversal shift in deaf and hearing kindergarten children. Unpublished master's thesis, Catholic University of America, 1964.

Schooley, M. and Hartman, G. W. Role of insight in the learning of logical relationships. *Amer. J. psychol.*, 1937, *49*, 287–292.

Skinner, B. F. *Verbal behavior*. New York: Appleton-Century-Crofts, 1957.

Staats, A. W. and Staats, Carolyn K. *Complex human behavior. A systematic extension of learning principles*. New York: Holt, Rinehart and Winston, 1963.

Teilhard de Chardin, P. *The phenomenon of man*. New York: Harper, 1959.

Templin, Mildred C. *Certain language skills in children*. Minneapolis: University of Minnesota Press, 1950.

Vygotsky, L. S. *Thought and language*. Cambridge: Massachusetts Institute of Technology Press, 1962.

Werner, H. and Kaplan, B. *Symbol formation. An organismic developmental approach to language and the expression of thought*. New York: Wiley, 1963.

Wertheimer, M. *Productive thinking*. New York: Harper, 1959.

Whorf, B. L. *Language, thought, and reality*. Cambridge: Massachusetts Institute of Technology Press, 1956.

Winitz, H. Relationships between language and nonlanguage measures of kindergarten children. *J. speech hear. res.*, 1959, *2*, 387–391.

Wohlwill, J. T. and Lowe, R. C. Experimental analysis of the development of the conservation of numbers. *Child develpm.*, 1962, *33*, 153–167.

Wrightstone, J. W., Aronow, Miriam S. and Moskowitz, Sue. Developing reading test norms for deaf children. *Test Service Bulletin, No. 98*. New York: Harcourt, Brace and World, 1962.

Youniss, J. Concept transfer as a function of shifts, age, and deafness. *Child develpm.*, 1964, *35*, 695–700.

Youniss, J. and Furth, H. G. Attainment and transfer of logical connectives in children. *J. educ. psychol.*, 1964, *55*, 357–361.

Index

233